WHY
LHASA DE SELA
MATTERS

Music Matters

Evelyn McDonnell

Series Editor

WHY LHASA DE SELA MATTERS

Fred Goodman

UNIVERSITY OF TEXAS PRESS
AUSTIN

Cover design: Amanda Weiss
Typeset in Knockout and Fournier
Book cover printed by Phoenix Color, interior by Sheridan Books.

Requests for permission to reproduce material
from this work should be sent to:

Permissions
University of Texas Press
P.O. Box 7819
Austin, TX 78713-7819
utpress.utexas.edu/rp-form

♾ The paper used in this book meets the minimum requirements of
ANSI/NISO Z39.48-1992 (R1997) (Permanence of Paper).

Library of Congress Cataloging-in-Publication Data
Names: Goodman, Fred, author.
Title: Why Lhasa De Sela matters / Fred Goodman.
Other titles: Music matters.
Description: Austin : University of Texas Press, 2019. | Series: Music matters
Identifiers: LCCN 2019013074
ISBN 978-1-4773-1962-8 (pbk. : alk. paper)
ISBN 978-1-4773-1963-5 (library e-book)
ISBN 978-1-4773-1964-2 (nonlibrary e-book)
Subjects: LCSH: Lhasa, 1972-2010. | Singers—Biography.
Classification: LCC ML420.L5359 G66 2019 | DDC 782.42164092 [B] —dc23
LC record available at https://lccn.loc.gov/2019013074

doi:10.7560/319628

For Alexandra

CONTENTS

PROLOGUE

January 9, 2010, New York

"Here's Lhasa, who died New Year's Day in Montreal."

That's how Jeannie Hopper introduced me to Lhasa de Sela.

Jeannie hosted *Liquid Sound Lounge*, a not-to-be-missed Saturday evening show on WBAI in New York, and I always counted on hearing several good records that I didn't know. I'm not sure what I expected after that introduction, but it wasn't this: a cold, shivering shimmer of bells and wind chimes and a low, rhythmic rumble like the voice of the earth that I previously had heard only in the music of Tibet's Gyuto Monks. Over it, a Don Cherry–inspired trumpet solo floated like a dry desert wind. We were someplace far away and unforgiving, someplace alien and elemental, following an ancient, difficult path under a giant night sky. Yet, the singer, who was both breathless and young, betrayed no fear or trepidation. If anything, she was an adventurer—and a philosopher in the bargain:

You've traveled this long
You just have to go on
Don't even look back to see

How far you've come
Though your body is bending
Under the load
There is nowhere to stop
Anywhere on this road.

It was mesmerizing and ambitious, musically sophisticated and emotionally advanced—the most intelligent pop record I had heard in a very long time. Lhasa? How could I have not heard of her? How could any artist capable of *this* die quiet and unknown? Perhaps, I thought, this record, "Anywhere on This Road," was a fluke—an inspired over-reach in an otherwise pedestrian career.

Either way, I needed to hear more. It's said that seeing is believing, but listening has always been my most reliable route to knowing, so the next morning I went digging for the song's album, *The Living Road*. It took just a verse of its opening track, "Con Toda Palabra" ("With Every Word"), an explicit and passionately sung ballad about being not just lovestruck but completely inflamed with desire, to know that what I had heard the night before was no fluke. Lhasa de Sela could sing and Lhasa de Sela could feel—and Lhasa de Sela had been for real. I had to know who she was and why I had never heard her music.

I soon learned that the American-born singer had been thirty-seven when she lost a grievous struggle with breast cancer. And I would also learn that, though she was unfamiliar to me and most Americans, Lhasa was a star in Canada and much of Europe, having earned a gold record and Juno Awards by absorbing and synthesizing such diverse strains as Gypsy music and flamenco, Mexican *rancheras*, Americana and jazz, Portuguese fado, Middle Eastern pop songs, Russian lullabies, *chanson française*, and South American folk melodies into her own unique and remarkable work. Over a thirteen-year recording career, she made just three albums: the first was in Spanish; the second, in Spanish, French, and English; and the last, exclusively in English. Lhasa's second album, *The Living Road*, won her the 2005 BBC Radio 3 World Music Award for Best Artist of the Americas and the *Times* of London named it one of the ten best world music albums of the decade.

Celebrated abroad, she has remained unknown in the United States. American record companies, quick to recognize her talent and license her work, proved nowhere near as adept at promoting Lhasa and introducing her to listeners. Her biggest bar to American success was obvious: approximately half of the limited number of recordings she had made weren't in English—a deal-breaker in a country where most of us aren't used to being asked to step outside the familiar walls of our Anglophone mass culture. But her linguistic choices don't hinder comprehension: as with poems, Lhasa's songs convey feeling before the meaning is fully grasped.

The shameful irony is that her consciousness was wholly American—daring and iconoclastic for sure, extraordinarily far-reaching and humanistic, but still homegrown.

I suspect she was this country's first world music chanteuse, and it bothered her deeply not to be heard here. It isn't just her big ears for eclectic music that make Lhasa and her records singular. There is also a rare thoughtfulness and wide-eyed sensuality in her work. She saw the world as imbued with magic and romance and a cosmic design— a dramatic and poetic outlook she expressed with wit and lyricism.

But Lhasa was also a bootstrap intellectual. The child of an unorthodox family, she had been urged from an early age to both take herself seriously and treat life as an adventure, and she responded by adopting punishingly high standards and expectations. An obsessive and deep reader, she turned an insatiable philosophic bent toward life's unanswerable questions, and that search became the wellspring of her songs. In her use of three languages one senses both a frustration with and a reach for deeper and more exact meanings, as if our day-to-day language doesn't quite get it done. Yet, her sophistication was leavened with romanticism and humor and made fresh by a naïf's ability to experience the world with unreserved wonder; she remained incapable of being jaded.

Lhasa's premature death notwithstanding, her three albums constitute a diary of a life's search and a full artistic journey. To put it plainly, I believe she was a significant artist who should be recognized and this book seeks to rectify that. But the work isn't the only arresting aspect of her story: Lhasa was not just an artist but also a true *bohème*. She lived a creative, romantic, uncompromising, and brave life.

Her hippie family lived much of the time in a converted school bus, crisscrossing between the United States and Mexico. Lhasa grew up without a telephone or television, and she was homeschooled by her parents, who rejected the bulk of material and social assumptions of mainstream American life. At the same time, they were fierce about instilling in their children an unquenchable curiosity, a deep devotion to spiritual and intellectual advancement, and the veneration of creativity. And because they succeeded, Lhasa would always remain somewhat estranged from society at large and a loner at heart, unable in particular to fathom the lack of curiosity and discipline in so many of the people she met. Hers was, to borrow a phrase from Emmett Grogan, a life played for keeps. For those of us who have fantasized about living such a life, ignoring conventions and having the courage to be that kind of parent, Lhasa's extraordinary story is romantic and inspiring.

It also, however, sounds a cautionary note as to what that choice can cost. Seeking freedom on the margins, the family lived an exhilarating but financially and emotionally precarious existence. They were ever on the move and ever on the edge. The consequences were a jarring lack of permanence, an element of real danger—strange people, strange surroundings, little in the way of a safety net—and an enduring feeling of isolation and otherness. That experience, coupled with a family legacy of hurt, strife, and tragedy that predated her birth, would weave the blue threads of sadness and insecurity into Lhasa's personality. And when the once tight-knit fabric of that family tore apart—the only world she knew—the anger and pain from that rip never completely mended.

Lhasa's friends and musical collaborators tell stories of a singularly enchanting and intense person, the once-in-a-lifetime friend who could be hilarious or dark, both child-like and dauntingly complex—an unendingly creative and deep-thinking woman who giggled like a young girl but could be rough on the people she loved and brutal to herself. As her music attests, she felt life intensely and was both enraptured by the mystery and deeply bruised by the realities of love. When diagnosed with cancer, Lhasa struggled to comprehend it and seemed lost. I believe what she felt was betrayal—as doubtless any person cut down before their time might—but a betrayal made that much more shocking and awful by her unquestioning faith in and excitement about the magic of life, a magic she had turned herself inside out to capture, shape, and share in hundreds of deeply focused and surprisingly intimate performances and three transcendent, death-denying albums.

A sorceress of the soul, Lhasa conjured the unknowable and the amazing, and in her all-too-brief life, she became the medium of that message. "There was always this mystery," says Arthur H, a French musician who was one of her close friends, "this damn mystery that was there because of her intensity."

Welcome to the mystery.

WHY
LHASA DE SELA
MATTERS

— 1 —

A FLOCK OF BLACK SHEEP

Children know perfectly well that unicorns aren't real,
but they also know that books about unicorns,
if they are good books, are true books.

URSULA K. LE GUIN,
"Why Are Americans Afraid of Dragons?"

Stephen Young was Woodstock's hippie doctor. Like so many others, he had wandered into the Catskills' famous bohemian art colony in the late 1960s, looking for something different. Young soon opened a general practice with an office on Mink Hollow Road and could count among his patients some of the community's most successful musicians, including members of the Band. But in 1972, when Dr. Benjamin Spock's 1946 manual *Baby and Child Care* was still the American bible for expectant parents, Young was perhaps best known around town for his unusual willingness to attend home births.

Among those Young agreed to assist was a family squatting in an old building at 6 Rock City Road. The expectant parents, Alejandro and Alexandra, had two young daughters and had connected with Young through Family of Woodstock, an alternative outreach and crisis intervention center based in the rambling Victorian house across the street at 5 Rock City Road. "We went to Woodstock looking for a community and to be part of the Woodstock Free Nation," said Alejandro Sela de Obarrio, who had landed a job at a macrobiotic restaurant. That summer, when the town condemned and sealed their squat to demolish the building and create a bank parking lot, the family purchased a small school bus and began camping nearby. In September, with the baby's birth imminent, Alejandro and Alexandra rented an unused Catskills Mountains ski cabin off Route 28 in Big Indian, twenty-five miles northwest of Woodstock, and summoned the doctor.

Young traveled surprisingly light, even by hippie standards. Pulling up to the cabin in a blue van with a friend to assist him, the doctor wore overalls and a straw hat, but no shirt. Instead of a stethoscope and satchel, he carried a gallon of Gallo burgundy. "He recommended that Alexandra drink a lot of it so it would be easier," Alejandro said. "And said it would be easier for him if he drank some, too." They sat outside and did just that until contractions were so close together that Alexandra had to go in and lie down. It proved an uncomplicated birth. It was the fifth daughter for Alexandra, who had been married previously. They wrapped the baby in a blanket and, in lieu of a cradle, placed her in a dresser drawer. "She was a beautiful, healthy child," says Alejandro.

Flush with pleasure, the proud new papa stepped outside and found a pay phone at a tavern across the road to share the good news with his father in Mexico City. The reaction proved a bit less than he had hoped for. "Another girl?" the incredulous grandfather asked. "This is your third girl. Unless you can have a male child, don't call me again—and especially not collect!" Stung, Alejandro could later recall the conversation with a laugh. "That's no news! Keep it to yourself!"

A few days after the baby's birth, the idyll ended when the police came to the cabin and arrested Alejandro. The charge was driving an unregistered vehicle. The family had been living in the area for thirty-one days and under local law—Big Indian is a hamlet within the town of Shandaken—residents had thirty days to register a vehicle in New York. The school bus, sporting Vermont plates and a "McGovern for President" bumper sticker, was impounded.

Brought before the judge, a surprised Alejandro offered to correct what was obviously a minor bureaucratic snafu. "I have a newborn baby," he explained. "I'll get to re-registering it."

The judge shared a smile with the arresting officer before leaning across the bench to Alejandro. "We really don't want you here," he said, adding that the town was not going to become a hippie haven like Woodstock. "We want you people to leave."

The bus was released back to Alejandro and Alexandra. They packed up their three young daughters, Ayin,

Sky, and the still-unnamed baby, and drove to Mexico. It wasn't until five months later that Alexandra finally found a name she felt suited her newest daughter. Having read Timothy Leary's popular handbook on LSD, *The Psychedelic Experience: A Manual Based on the Tibetan Book of the Dead*, she and Alejandro then moved on to tackle the original Buddhist tome that inspired Leary. Along with providing a spiritual guide to navigating *bardo*, the state between death and rebirth in which a Buddhist's consciousness sits suspended, the book told of the holy city of Lhasa, built high on the Tibetan plateau. The name means "place of the gods," and somehow, those rarified heights and aspirations felt like an appropriate christening and wish.

"They were incapable of having a middle-class life," Lhasa de Sela would say years later when asked about her mother and father. "Their parents were well-off, but they were the black sheep of their families. They took a lot of hallucinogenic drugs and took incredible risks."[1]

Those risks—and the life her parents chose—would have a profound impact on Lhasa. And just as affecting were the dramatic and painful histories Alejandro and Alexandra were fleeing—a legacy of family disputes and tragedies occurring before Lhasa's birth but destined to play out again not just in her music but also in the way she would live her life.

* * *

It was at the Actor's Studio in New York that Elena Karam met the director Elia Kazan and landed her most notable film role, playing the mother in Kazan's 1963 critically acclaimed autobiographical immigrant saga, *America, America*. Offscreen, Karam had a daughter, Alexandra, with Norman Schur, a New York attorney. Schur, an unusual and brilliant man, would practice trust and estates law in both New York and London for fifty years and then launch a second career as an author, lexicographer, and leading expert on the differences in English language usage in the United States and Great Britain. But he only married Elena to give their daughter a name; the couple divorced shortly thereafter and never lived together. In 1948, when Alexandra was seven years old, Elena married the enormously successful public relations executive John Hill, who built his firm, Hill & Knowlton, into the first modern and perhaps most influential corporate imaging and political strategy consulting company in the United States. Among Hill's clients were oil companies, the tobacco industry, and Richard Nixon's presidential campaign.

Though her stepfather legally adopted Alexandra and provided an affluent lifestyle, replete with country homes and an Upper East Side apartment in Manhattan, she was extremely unhappy and her teen years were a nightmare. "My mother was not easy," Alexandra says. "She had suffered a lot in her own childhood and became a person who was rather cruel, even sadistic." Her relationship with her stepfather, whom she loathed—personally at first and later for the causes and clients he championed—was horrendous. "I was difficult and angry," Alexandra says.

If hard to control, she was also precocious, artistic, and intellectually gifted. A painstaking photographer whose published work shows an extraordinary eye and unfailing sensitivity to contrast, she dropped out of high school but studied poetry with Stanley Kunitz at the New School. A music fanatic, she learned to play the harp. But when she began to act out and get in trouble, Hill wanted no part of it. "I was an embarrassment to him—Mr. Hill & Knowlton. He told my mother, 'I can't have this—you've got to get rid of her.'" At sixteen, Alexandra was shipped off to Chestnut Lodge, the mental hospital in Rockville, Maryland, memorialized in the novel *I Never Promised You a Rose Garden*. "In part, my mother thought she was doing the right thing—or trying to—and though I wasn't crazy, I was put in a mental hospital because that's what people often did at the time with kids they didn't know what to do with."

Alexandra soon saw that the plan was to keep her hospitalized indefinitely. She decided to foil it. "I walked into the nurse's station and read the files and realized they kept people there forever. I also saw that that was fine with my mother." Unaware that she was sleeping with one of her caretakers, the hospital deemed Alexandra's behavior good enough to award her privileges: she was allowed to have pocket money and to take occasional shopping trips into town. "I saved my money and took a train to New York

City and stayed with a friend." Her Rockville inamorato joined her, and they were married as soon as she turned eighteen—a relationship that lasted just eighteen months but served a purpose. "I was afraid they were going to try and put me back in the hospital," she admits. "I just didn't want them to have control over me anymore."

Separated, Alexandra met and fell in love with bassist Charlie Haden, then part of saxophonist Ornette Coleman's revolutionary jazz group in residence at the Five Spot in Greenwich Village. It was an exciting time and scene that left a lifelong impression. Alexandra was in the studio for the December 1960 recording of Coleman's landmark experimental album *Free Jazz: A Collective Improvisation*, which featured two quartets playing simultaneously—one led by Coleman and the other by Eric Dolphy and Freddie Hubbard. She also picked up a heroin habit. "I separated from Charlie because I wanted to stop," she says.

Alexandra moved to Mexico and kicked her habit. She also met and married Alphonso de la Vega, a brilliant and flamboyant designer who had his own demons, including a violent streak. Following the birth of two daughters, Gabriela and Samantha, the couple split up, and Alexandra, despite a fraught relationship with her mother, returned to New York with the girls to try her hand at acting. Lonely and uncertain, she slipped back into dope. "It was just rough being alone in the city with the little ones," she says.

Elena, now separated from Hill—he cited Alexandra's wild, embarrassing behavior as the reason—had taken two apartments in the Dakota, the famed apartment building at Central Park West and Seventy-Second Street that was later home to John Lennon and Yoko Ono. Along with the apartment Elena occupied, there was a former maid's quarters upstairs on the ninth floor. Alexandra and the girls moved into that tiny apartment, and it was here that their lives took a horrifying and momentous turn.

"It was a two-room apartment with a tiny kitchen and a microscopic bath. There was a living room and bedroom, where the two girls were, and there were bars two-thirds of the way up the windows. I was in the bathroom washing out diapers and came back into the room just in time to see Sammy go out over the top of the bars. I saw her go out."

The toddler tumbled two floors to a slanting roof on the seventh floor, landing in a rain gutter, where a metal support impaled her cheek. By luck, a woman living on the seventh floor happened to be in a rarely used storeroom that opened to the gutter and she pulled Samantha in before she fell again.

The child received plastic surgery to repair her face, and Elena began legal proceedings to have the girls taken away from Alexandra. "My mother decided it was my fault because I wasn't in the room. Actually, what I was guilty of and the reason the girls were taken away from me is that I was strung out on heroin. I understood and understand that."

At that time, under the Rockefeller Plan, suspected addicts in New York could be forced to submit to a medical examination on short notice and, if found to be using, incarcerated for one to three years. "My mother did that to me," Alexandra says. "I got the notice on a Friday and was supposed to appear on Monday."

Elena had already put Gabriela and Samantha with caretakers in the country, and Alexandra feared losing them for good. "I found out where Sammy and Gabby were and I went there and told them I'd like to see the kids and take them out for an afternoon. We got on a train, went to the airport, and I wrote a bad check and took a plane to Mexico and kicked with no particular help and two young girls."

Desperate for assistance, she returned to Alphonso in Puerto Vallarta, only to discover that he was more violent than ever. After suffering a savage beating, Alexandra had him locked up overnight so that she could take the girls to Guadalajara and begin formal divorce proceedings. "Because I married him in Mexico, I had to stay there to divorce him. I found out he knew where I was and that's when I made my big mistake. I wanted the girls to be safe so I asked my mother to come down and take them to the States." And she did.

It was while living in Guadalajara and waiting for her divorce to come through that Alexandra met Alejandro Sela.

Like Alexandra, he had had an unsettled and unsettling childhood. Born in San Francisco at the end of World War II, Alejandro spent the early years of his life shuffling between Mexico and the United States. His mother, Carmen de Obarrio, was a Panamanian concert pianist who had recorded for RCA Victor in the 1920s. She was born into one of the founding families that helped the United States split Panama from Colombian rule to facilitate the building of the Panama Canal. And while his maternal grandfather had served as Panama's envoy to Washington, Alejandro's childhood was far from grand. His father, also named Alejandro, was a Mexican businessman and Carmen's junior by twenty years. He found San Francisco unwelcoming and they returned to Mexico. "We couldn't get our foot in the door," Alejandro recalled. "My father's English was poor and he couldn't find a job with the soldiers returning." Four years later, they tried California again, moving in with Alejandro's grandmother in Alameda. He attended school there for the next seven years, learning English. But his life changed again in 1956 when his parents divorced. He found himself back in Mexico City, living in a hotel with his mother on child support checks. Though Carmen soon had a new and even younger husband, she was always short of money and taught piano to make ends meet, leaving Alejandro in the nominal care of the hotel's bellboy and desk clerk. He took to wandering the streets of Mexico City, "hanging out with the downtown kids and going astray."

"My mother really couldn't handle me," he says, "and was so financially hard-pressed that she could hardly afford me." By fifteen, he was essentially homeless. "She gave me my papers and all the money she had in her wallet and said she would pray for me. And she did. I knocked around for a couple of years on my own."

After two years, he reconnected with his father, who had subsequently become a successful industrialist, and finished high school at a Methodist boarding school in Laredo, Texas. The plan was for Alejandro to return to Mexico City to attend college and work in his father's factory. "He had become the king of Styrofoam in Central America— he introduced this marvelous material there and made everything out of it: floatation devices, coolers, Christmas decorations." And though Alejandro briefly attended the University of the Americas, he couldn't see himself going into the business or living with his father and stepmother. "So I dropped out."

By 1967, Alejandro was back in the States, just in time for the Summer of Love. "I was in the Bay Area for about a year and then traveled back to Mexico to kind of hip all my Mexican brothers to all I'd been turned on to in the Bay Area," he says. "The revolution and the new world."

Encouraged by the promise of a counterculture, Alejandro would became an earnest and lifelong seeker of a spiritual life—a path that would have a huge impact on the lives and views of his children.

"My father basically tried every single religion that exists on the planet," says Miriam de Sela, Lhasa's younger sister. "And had no qualms about going from one to the next—to him, it was not contradictory. In fact, it was all working one with the other and making perfect sense to him to be chanting Buddhist prayers and have his rosary for the Hail Mary and go up on a hill and meditate. And it went on and on and on. Constantly. And actually, in a way he still does that."

While singing with a band in Guadalajara, the Stone Façade, Alejandro and a friend made a pilgrimage to the Oaxacan village of Huautla de Jiménez in search of the shaman, María Sabina. A renowned *curandera*, or medicine woman, Sabina had gained fame ten years earlier when American banker and amateur mycologist R. Gordon Wasson published an article in *Life* chronicling how, in seeking to separate fact from legend regarding pre-Columbian rituals associated with a magic mushroom the Aztecs called *teonanacatl*, or "God's flesh," he happened across Sabina. In an all-night spiritual ceremony, or *velada*, that combined Mazatec and Catholic teachings, she had guided Wasson as he tripped on the psychedelic mushroom *Psilocybe mexicana*.[2] Though unable to find Sabina, Alejandro did locate another village *curandero*. During their *velada*, the shaman counseled the young men to find women and raise families; at the band's next rehearsal, Alejandro met Alexandra. She was five years his senior—worldly, arrestingly beautiful, and impressive as hell.

"She was streetwise and had really been around," he says. "Also, as spiritual seekers we shared a lot of interests in things like philosophy, Buddhism, and comparative religion. She was very well read and turned me on to some things. I was taken by her wisdom."

Alexandra was soon pregnant with the couple's first daughter, Ayin, and wrote to Elena to say she was settled and ready to take Gabriela and Samantha back. The response stunned her: Elena had been granted custody of the girls and Alexandra was legally barred from contact. "If you get anywhere near them, you'll be arrested," Elena warned her.

Elena believed taking charge of the girls was in their best interest. But as Alexandra could attest—and as her own daughters would soon painfully discover—motherhood wasn't exactly Elena's strong suit. To the extent that she actually raised the girls, it was at arm's length. The sisters were split up, shuttled from caretaker to caretaker, boarding school to boarding school. Some of the situations proved abusive.

"Grandma's instincts were not for the maternal," says Gabriela. "Whatever her intentions, she was an incredibly destructive person and very controlling. She had all this money from marrying my grandfather and a lot of power over what happened to people in the family. She would decide from year to year where Sammy and I were going to be and just change her mind, thinking she was being loving and doing the right thing. But she rarely did the right thing. If you look back on it, it's crazy. One year one place, another the next. That's a pretty powerful thing to do, to take custody of the kids and not even keep them, just move them around."

Elena proved a disastrous mother and guardian. In addition to Alexandra, Elena had adopted and raised a nephew born out of wedlock, Wiley. He drank himself to death at thirty-six. Samantha, who was also moved from place to place and school to school, would later have her own problems with heroin. "Grandma was the architect of all our childhoods," says Gabriela. "She almost got three out of the four of us. We barely made it—and Wiley didn't."

The relationship between Elena and Alexandra was particularly fraught. "She basically denied my mother for the rest of her life," Gabriela says. "I know there are reasons, but a lot of Grandma's choices were strange and that colored the rest of the family. When my mother visited, she would make her leave her kids in the guesthouse, and only then could my mother come visit her in the main house. She wanted all the attention and didn't want my mother distracted by her own children. You have to understand: the kids born after me and Sammy—Ayin, Sky, Lhasa, Miriam, and Mischa—had a very different experience of my mother. When we were taken away from her, our mother was destroyed, she was changed forever. They got a different person."

Though happier and more comfortable in Mexico than the United States, Alexandra was intent on reclaiming Gabriela and Samantha. "She was very anxious to redeem her two children," says Alejandro. With the newborn Ayin in tow, they left Mexico City on what would be the first of several quests back and forth to New York. They settled in Staten Island because Alexandra feared her mother would have her arrested if she lived too close. Their bid to regain custody of the older girls failed, but it was here that another daughter, Sky, was born. They returned to Mexico, then, in 1972, ventured again to New York in another futile bid for Gabby and Sam. That same year, Lhasa was born. The family moved back to Mexico. Then, when Lhasa was six, they again departed Guadalajara for New York. They were living a precarious hand-to-mouth life—sometimes dangerously so.

"Alexandra and I were both very intent on self-realization and finding God," Alejandro says. "And one of the ways of finding God was to put yourself in dire straits and wait for miraculous intervention. And in that way get in touch with the maker and provider. That's a really scary thing to do, especially if you have little children. And it wasn't very wise of us to do so. But we did it."

Indigent, the family found a home at the Catholic Worker Farm in Tivoli, New York. The Catholic Worker Movement was founded in Manhattan in 1933 by Dorothy Day, a Marxist journalist who had converted to Catholicism, and Peter Maurin, a theologian pursuing a life of Christlike poverty on skid row. The Movement is committed to nonviolence, voluntary poverty, and works of mercy. The Tivoli farm was just one of hundreds of Catholic Worker communities and hospitality houses established over the years to serve the homeless, the hungry, and those seeking a spiritual commitment. For Alejandro, the Movement and the farm were an ideal fit.

"We had always been looking for a community and to try a communal existence and we did there," he says. "And we were very happily engaged in politics, in studying comparative religions, doing communal activism, and meeting a lot of people. It was very anarchistic." Just as important, the farm's philosophy regarding work dovetailed neatly with his own: having turned his back on his father's offer to take over the Styrofoam factory, Alejandro was determined to be a laborer. "I was filled with Marxist ideas of doing real work and wanted to be a member of the proletariat," he says. In Tivoli, work was handled communally and Alejandro cooked once a week, milked the goats, and worked in the garden; his main job was as a driver.

Though they lived together in a single room in a cold, unheated derelict dubbed the "Mansion," the family's two years on the farm were happy. And during that time, Alexandra and Alejandro welcomed their fourth daughter, Miriam, her birth unassisted by doctors. "It was just the three of us," says Alejandro.

Dorothy Day's health declined in 1978, and the farm was soon sold. "They got a much smaller place and the people who took over after Dorothy did not find us to be their type of people and told us we had to be on our way," says Alexandra. "That was fine; it was good to move on." They decamped to Towners, New York, a tiny town an hour north of New York City where John Hill had owned a country house with a barn on one hundred acres. Upon her ex-husband's death in 1977, Elena had been pleasantly surprised to discover he had never finalized their divorce. Now a rich woman, she allowed the de Selas to stay there.

After two years in the unheated Mansion, the Towners property was like a luxurious new planet. Located in the foothills of the Catskills, the land was nearly pristine and, along with the two-story, four-bedroom main house, included an apartment in the barn, a small caretaker's cabin, and an old swimming pool. "Here we are in this big house," says Alexandra. "After living together in one room, the girls are all excited about having their own rooms." But that night, once everyone had snuggled into their soft, warm beds, they heard someone walking up and down the stairs. "This was not creaking," Alexandra insists. "This was footsteps. And, of course, there was nobody there!" When the footfalls resumed the next night, everyone abandoned their new privacy in favor of sleeping together again in one room. Eventually, they moved to the smaller cabin.

Despite never attending school, the girls learned to read at an early age. For basic education the family used Calvert, a traditional correspondence course for home schooling, with Alexandra doing the lion's share of the teaching. "We were very disciplined about doing school every day," says Alejandro.

Indeed, if Alexandra and Alejandro had an overriding pedagogy, it was to encourage curiosity, creativity, and confidence. "Papa and Mama were both very demanding," says Sky de Sela. "And I say that as a compliment. They demanded of us that we be bright, that we be alive and curious and apply ourselves to whatever we were going to do. They both felt education was something very sacred and you don't mess around with it. And creativity? Whew! If somebody would give us a television, they'd throw it away. *Nope, we're not doing that—we're doing this other thing.* And each person could do a different thing; they didn't structure us, but encouraged in a deep way. They had a belief in a rebellious mode of life and did not want to take part in a lot of what they believed to be somehow plastic. Some people would look at our family and think we were just a crazy bunch of hippies with no structure in our lives at all, but it had a kind of rigorous quality to it."

Raised without a telephone or television, the de Sela daughters would all mimic their parents as avid readers and independent thinkers. They also became autodidacts, capable of intense focus and, in later years, training so strict as to be punishing. (In one of the more dramatic demonstrations of familial self-discipline, Samantha quit heroin by becoming an ultramarathoner.) Friends who knew Lhasa as an adult were struck by the breadth of her education and the depth of her reading, considering that her formal schooling was sporadic and included just one semester of college.

"I've rarely met people who went to university who had her general knowledge," says her friend, Lousnak Abdalian. "Because of her home schooling, she knew how to study and had this way of knowing that she had to go every day and get knowledge—she was self-taught and daily. She went to her neighborhood library every day and whenever I went to her house, she had a new book to show me. She believed very, very strongly that this is how you become a better person tomorrow than you are today."

There were, however, downsides. Raised as an outsider and accustomed to impermanence, Lhasa learned to rely only on herself and her family—an impulse that affected virtually all her relationships for the rest of her life. Most parents play a large role in shaping a child's personality and direction, but, in Lhasa's case, that influence was enormous and nearly exclusive. Her isolated childhood essentially presented her with only two models of adult behavior, both intense and not always easy to reconcile: her father's austere search for enlightenment and perfection versus a creative, adventurous, and unapologetically combustible mother.

Invariably, if the family put out the tendrils of tentative roots, local authorities would insist on enrolling the girls in school. After spending the fall and winter in Towners, the de Selas were visited in April by a representative from the local school board who insisted the girls be in school for placement tests the following week. When the tests showed they were well ahead of their grades, Alexandra simply declined to enroll them, telling the school board the family was heading to California in the coming months.

That summer, the de Selas hitched a beat-up '66 Rambler to the back of their school bus and drove from New

York to Sacramento. Alejandro's continuing spiritual quest had led him to the Old Catholic Church, an obscure group founded in Switzerland in the mid-nineteenth century that initially split with Rome over the doctrine of papal infallibility. Since then, its handful of American congregants had come to embrace a wide range of worship, including prayers to Yoruba saints, séances for channeling spirits, and even the occasional exorcism. One of the Church's primary attractions for Alejandro was that it allowed its priests to marry and have families. He sought training and ordination.

Settling the family at a KOA campground, Alejandro became acolyte to an Old Catholic Church priest, Brother Luke. The priest, however, was experiencing his own spiritual crisis and soon opted to close the Sacramento Mission to pursue a monastic life in Holland. The Church sent Alejandro to Salinas to train with another priest, Brother Joe. But getting to Salinas proved an adventure: in Elk Grove, just outside of Sacramento, the bus engine blew up. The family had no money for a tow, so the police pushed them to a nearby Exxon station. The gas station owner let them spend the night.

The next morning Alejandro found work picking melons. When the farmer, a Mormon, came back to meet Alejandro's family at their gas station bivouac, he found the two older girls helping Alexandra wash diapers in the station's bathroom sink while Lhasa swept the bus. Moved by their plight, he gave Alejandro a carful of watermelons to sell on the street in Sacramento. One customer proved to be an auto mechanic and Good Samaritan. He showed Alejandro how to locate a replacement engine in a junkyard and then spent the next three weeks helping him rebuild it in his off-time. The girls, who studied with Alexandra in the mornings, worked picking tomatoes in the afternoons.

In late September, when Lhasa turned eight, there was a party at the bus: guests included the melon farmer and his family, the mechanic and his family, and the gas station owner. It was a Raggedy Ann-themed affair—Alexandra made Lhasa a doll, while her older sisters crafted a piñata, and the mechanic's wife and kids brought a Raggedy Ann cake—and Lhasa, as an adult, would tag it as her most memorable birthday. For Alejandro, it proved a bittersweet memory, a "wonderful and pitiful occasion. Wonderful that Alex was so long-suffering and that the girls were so unspoiled and appreciative," he would later write, "wonderful that the bus was almost ready to roll, pitiful that, as the father of this family, I had exposed us to deprivation and the humiliation of being hassled by the police, pitied by the station owner, and tolerated by the community."[3]

Finally arriving in Salinas, they all moved into a spare bedroom in Brother Joe's home. A high school science teacher, he administered his mission out of the house, having converted a two-car garage into the chapel of St. Michael Archangel, complete with altar, stained glass win-

dows, and rows of folding chairs. For the next couple of
months, Alejandro worked days, cultivating mums and
baby's breath at a cut-flower farm, and studying with the
priest in his off-time. The arrangement unraveled, however, over Brother Joe's growing conviction that Alexandra, who was not shy about expressing her emotions and
could be volatile, was a woman in need of an exorcism.

"He decided I was the root of all evil," she says with a
laugh, "and something had to be done in that department.
I did not cooperate. We ended up having to leave."

The family returned to the school bus, perhaps their tru-
est home.

The bus was where the girls were most separated from
the world at large, the place where the differences between
their parents' choices and values and those of society were
ever evident. "In our family, we grew up *so* alienated from
normal life—in the sense of social construct—that we fell
back on ourselves," says Samantha, whose grandmother
eventually allowed her and Gabriela to travel through California and Mexico with their mother and sisters. "There
was no other way to go but in."

The hand-to-mouth wandering of their childhood and
the sense of separateness would define them and become an
unbreakable soul bond of experience: as an adult, Lhasa did
not conceive of herself as the third of four sisters so much
as one in a set of quadruplets. Indeed, to see Ayin, Sky,
Lhasa, and Miriam together is to witness variations on a
theme: what's most dominant and defining in one sister—

physically, emotionally, cognitively—is observable to some lesser degree in any of the others. You hear Alexandra in the way each thinks and speaks, and they share the same goofy, unspoiled laugh.

"Our sisterhood was hermetic," says Sky. "We really depended on each other. We always knew that we were going to lose everybody except each other. Kids can get used to anything. And they do. And we did. We got it after a while: we could have a really wonderful time with someone and feel an incredible connection and then never see them again in our lives. Or we could have a really strong connection to a place and feel like that was the place we needed to be, and then leave. We didn't have a lot of control, obviously, as kids. And we had to accept this wonderful and often difficult reality: there was impermanence. That wasn't just a concept for us. It was reality. That's why we relied on each other: we needed each other."

It wasn't always soul-searching—sometimes it was just childhood. "Lhasa was the one the girls picked on," says Samantha. "She wanted to be a part of things and Ayin and Sky would kick her out because she was the little brat who got the most attention from Mama. So Lhasa would make her fort under the blanket on the bunk in the back and go be lonely for a while. Then my Mom would chew the other girls out: 'C'mon! Be nice to Lhasa! Don't exclude her.' That was the bus thing."

To soothe herself and while away time, Lhasa would sing—sometimes ceaselessly. "She sang so much that her sisters, especially Ayin who was the eldest and strict, would say, 'Shut up, Lhasa! Stop SINGING! We just can't stand it anymore!'" says Alejandro. "And Lhasa would say okay— and start humming. She became very adept at humming and whistling because her sisters didn't want her to sing anymore."

The humming and whistling blossomed into something surprising.

"Lhasa composed her tunes in the weirdest way," says her friend, filmmaker Ralph Dfouni. "She whistled them. She really didn't know how to read or write music and she had to find a way to communicate the tunes that she had in her head to the musicians. And it was mostly by whistling and humming. I remember Lhasa whistling most of my life with her. Walking in the street, she's whistling; sitting on the couch, she's whistling; cooking, she's whistling. She whistles a lot. That was her instrument in a way."

The de Selas stopped in Castroville, the small farm town between Monterey and Santa Cruz that bills itself as "the Artichoke Center of the World." They rented a small house and stayed put for a bit. Alejandro took a job crating artichokes in a packing house. But even while enrolled in the local schools, the girls were expected to continue with their own interests and education.

"In my family, there is a certain pressure to be creative, a certain belief that life without creativity is wasted," Lhasa said. "In some families, it's money, or reputation, or respectability, or success. In my family, it's creativity.

We're a bit anxious, all of us, all the time, to produce some proof of our human worth. I have a joke with one of my sisters: 'What did you do today?' Oh, I woke up, ran a few miles, did my breathing exercises, worked on my novel, wrote a song, did some sketches, worked on learning Russian, had a breakfast of fruit and distilled water . . . but now I need to really get to work!"[4]

Afternoons were spent preparing to perform for their parents in the evening. There was a makeshift stage with a homemade curtain, and the sisters would huddle and plan their show. For Lhasa, it was improvising song-stories that combined music and fairy tales while Alexandra accompanied her on the harp.

Fairy tales had become a nearly obsessive interest as soon as Lhasa could read. Reading was a constant in the bus—"All we *ever* did was read," says Sky—and among the most pored-over books on the bus were the classic fairy and folk tales collected in Andrew Lang's peerless, twelve-volume series known as the fairy books of many colors.

A Scottish novelist, poet, and collector of hundreds of folk stories from all over the world, Lang began editing and re-telling them for children in 1889 with *The Blue Fairy Book* and completed his series twenty-one years later with *The Lilac Fairy Book*. Critically acclaimed and extremely popular at the time of publication, the lushly illustrated series appeared hopelessly old-fashioned by the television age and was largely and unjustly forgotten in the United States by the 1970s; they could be found for next to nothing on Salvation Army and Goodwill book shelves. Filled with enchantment stories and color plates of princes and princesses, quests, spells, and magic transformations, they became deeply embedded in Lhasa's lexicon.

"These were beautiful, important fairy tales," says Sky. "Very simple spiritual journeys. The collection was a mythology that became Lhasa's whole world."

"She loved fairy tales and was certainly imaginative," says Alejandro. "So she kind of confused fairy tales with her own circumstance growing up and in that light saw things imbued with a kind of magic and mystery and wonder."

"I wasn't just reading about magic and adventures," said Lhasa: "I was also living it. We were living in places with no electricity and you'd look up at night and see the Milky Way. Living with that presence changes you a lot— your life is much more magical. All of these strange intense experiences—living in trailer parks where there are really strange people and living kind of out on the edge. Living in peoples' driveways. Almost drowning in the ocean, stepping on a sea urchin."[5] Living without nets showed her that her life could—and perhaps should—be precarious. "I always have this image of the way things were one hundred, two hundred years ago: if you were a sailor you'd get on a boat and you'd sail away and didn't really know if you were ever going to come back."[6]

She was particularly smitten with stories of transformation: children changing magically back and forth into animals; impoverished but kind-hearted and adventurous girls found to be princesses; the once lost and maligned now regained and restored to honor.

"It's almost like she did look at the world as one big fairy tale," says Sarah Pagé, Lhasa's friend and musical collaborator. "She loved the idea of people and animals being integrated. This is so Lhasa: she said that when she was a kid she always dreamed of having antlers. She thought if she had antlers, she'd be so beautiful. And everybody would look at her, see her antlers, and realize how beautiful she was. Yeah," she adds with a laugh, "they would really suit her."[7]

Indeed, the fantasy was straight out of one of Lang's stories, "The Girl-Fish," in which an enchanted heroine on a quest goes through a series of animal transformations. While in the guise of an antlered deer, she proves so beguiling that a young prince falls hopelessly in love with her. Said Lhasa: "I think it's hard for kids to live with the kind of up-rootedness and insecurity we had. We attached ourselves onto the romance of it. That definitely has served me well. I have this sense that my life is a story that is not a sad story."[8]

Along with fairy tales, music was a childhood constant. But unlike her peers, Lhasa wasn't listening to the music on the radio or television, or the music that was popular at school. She was listening to what her parents brought with them on the bus—a delineation with a profound impact on her own tastes and musical choices. "I'm not very structured," says Alexandra, "I'm not very balanced. What

I provided was thousands of books and lots of music." Indeed, Alexandra, who had studied music and loved to sing, had exceptionally wide-ranging listening habits and managed to maintain a substantial collection of tapes and records, ranging from Maria Callas to field recordings, while Alejandro's records included traditional *rancheras* by Mexican singers like Cuco Sànchez and Chavela Vargas, as well as the work of Latin American political songwriters and performers, including Victor Jara and Violeta Parra.

Unaware that she was being exposed to anything out of the ordinary, Lhasa embraced it all in innocence. Taken by his songs and his photograph on an album, she imagined marrying Jara, unaware that he had been tortured and murdered in Chile for opposing Pinochet's military junta. "I grew up with all kinds of music without thinking that any of it was strange or extraordinary. It was normal to be listening to music from all over the world—South America, Mexico, a lot of black music, Bob Dylan, also Arab music, Gypsy music, Asian, and classical. When I first heard about 'world music,' I didn't know what they were talking about. It's just music to me."[9]

Castroville's charms soon wore thin. "The schools were absolutely awful," says Alexandra. "And in the spring we left for Mexico."

Returning to Guadalajara, they lived in a campground and Alejandro began picking up work as a language instructor, teaching English to Mexicans and Spanish to Americans. A newspaper ad seeking English teachers caught his attention. The Fundación Nacional de Turismo (National Tourism Board) needed teachers to train hotel workers in Los Cabos on the Baja Peninsula. Alexandra and Alejandro packed the kids and the bus onto the ferry and moved to San Jose de Los Cabos.

Now filled with vacation homes and popular resorts, the area was still empty and undeveloped in the early 1980s, more backwater than tourist haven. There was a single paved road—everything else was dirt—and the family settled in near the beach. Lhasa and her sisters loved it.

"It was an exhilarating and life-affirming thing we were allowed to live," says Sky. "I have such beautiful images— so many. A lot of good barefoot trees to climb in and the ocean and new languages and forced into a vibrant openness. And that was the good part. And the difficult part— there was no stability. Kids love stability. So do adults."

Having at last reached what seemed an idyllic outpost, family life should have settled down. Instead, it became increasing stormy as their parents' marriage first frayed and then imploded. Alejandro could be solemn and prideful while Alexandra, intense and unapologetically emotional, was capable of explosive scenes, especially when drinking. And as they argued with greater frequency and volume, day-to-day life grew increasingly unhappy. "I hate it when mom and dad yell at each other," eleven-year-old Sky wrote in her journal. "Why won't they stop?"[10] Soon they would. Alexandra moved out and into a nearby beach house with another man; Alejandro moved the bus up the hill for distance.

The breakup was devastating. As an adult, Ayin would recall an incident from the period in which she was badly scalded with boiling water but had only one thought: *now Mama will have to come back*. Lhasa, not yet a teenager, had an equally primal reaction: she found the shredding of the family fabric and Alexandra's rages both baffling and terrifying. If this was being a woman, she wanted no part of it. Her inability to integrate and accept those scenes would have a lifelong impact on her relationships, particularly with her mother and with men, and bring an almost inexplicable complexity and a touch of sadness to her life and personality. The spiritual and mystical longings and unabashed romanticism that characterized her songs were a true distillation of both her childhood environment and her most deeply felt yearnings and faith in possibilities. Yet, there was a darker, less sure, and more fearful part of her that was just as integral, just as much Lhasa. Often personally guarded, even a bit prudish, she feared losing control of her emotions and would have virtually no intimate relationships until well into her twenties.

A new arrangement saw the girls splitting the week between parents. It also meant the end of their home schooling. "When they were with me, I couldn't really be with the kids much because I was teaching every day," Alejandro says. "So I put them in school—there was a Catholic school."

Alejandro had also met Marybeth Pettit, a young American woman who had wandered down to Baja from Albany,

New York. She marveled at the surroundings—and these unusual children who had been exposed to so much. "You really felt like you were living in the Wild West," she says. "And the girls were totally unspoiled—just lovely. They perfected their Spanish there, walked to the school downtown. Lhasa really loved it there."

In September 1982, Alexandra was severely injured in an automobile accident. Sustaining seven broken ribs, pelvic damage, and head trauma, she actively hallucinated that she was Japanese and living in Japan with two dogs rather than in a Mexican hospital bed. Recovering and released after four months, she went to a rehabilitation hospital in San Francisco; in early 1983, she took an apartment at Haight and Divisadero Streets and came back to Baja to pick up Lhasa and Miriam. Ayin and Sky wanted to finish out the school year in Mexico, and Alejandro later brought them to San Francisco before heading back east with Marybeth.

It was a difficult transition for Lhasa. The girls were enrolled at the Urban School. Now a collegiate fast-track high school, it was something of a hippie school then, but even that felt strange and uncomfortable to Lhasa. After living in the family's bohemian cocoon, Lhasa found San Francisco to be huge and unnerving. Timid and unsure how to make friends, she remembered feeling "a bit like a lonely refugee. I was very shy, and I was actually pretty scared of people. It was a tough experience."[11] Constant humming was the best way to soothe and steady herself.

At Urban, Ayin and Sky found a profession suitably off the beaten path. Sky befriended Gypsy Snyder, a classmate whose own unorthodox parents ran the Pickle Family Circus. They, along with Miriam, were soon helping at the circus and developing skills that would lead to respective careers as a tightrope walker, a trapeze artist and clown, and a gymnast and tumbler. It wasn't for Lhasa, though, who seemed particularly unengaged.

"She was kind of lazy," says Samantha. "She was a bit chubby then and just laid around her room, which was messy. Ayin would get up and sweep the kitchen and clean the counters—she was annoyed that my mother wasn't doing it—but you could say to Lhasa, 'These are your chores' until you were blue in the face, and she just wouldn't do it."

Lhasa felt more at ease with her father, and when Alejandro and Marybeth settled in upstate New York, Lhasa opted to live with them one year, attending a public middle school near Albany. "That was a real eye-opener for her," says Marybeth. Until then, her family had just been her family—like anyone else's, if a bit unsettled. The experience forced Lhasa to confront just how unusual her parents were and how dramatically different their values and that upbringing had made her. Life on the margins had been precarious and emotionally stormy, lived cheek by jowl and close to the bone. Simultaneously, Alexandra and Alejandro had insisted through every rollercoaster turn that their children *must* take themselves seriously and be constantly searching inward: that they pursue knowledge, creativity, work, and spiritual values as if their very lives depend on it—because they do. Everything about Lhasa's new classmates made it evident that she had been set on a different road. "I'm amazed by people's lack of curiosity and lack of faith in life," she said.[12] It was a revelation that never ceased to shock her and her sisters.

"Lhasa had an intense curiosity and that runs in the family—I can see it with my own children," says Miriam. "I started circus when I was 9 and no one was telling me that I had to do that. We were self-willed and motivated and *incredibly* serious. What was really passed to us in the way we were raised is that it's an interior search: *advancing, advancing, advancing*. Every time we've been in contact with any "normal" institution, it's shocking. At the risk of sounding rude, I teach circus classes to children and my jaw drops every time because they're terrible students. They don't listen and seem to think it's possible to negotiate all things at all times."

With her sisters already enraptured with circus, it seemed Lhasa had wandered into an Albany cul-de-sac. Bored and at a loss for anything to do one night, she sat down on the couch with Marybeth, who was watching a PBS documentary on the jazz singer Billie Holiday. Lhasa sat silent and wide-eyed through the documentary, mesmerized not just by Holiday's music but also by the romance and tragedy of the chanteuse's life. As the credits rolled, she turned to Marybeth and pointed at the screen.

"That's what I'm going to do."

— 2 —

THE WAILING WOMAN

Because they are uncertain,
they put on the bold
looks of experience.

WILLIAM CARLOS WILLIAMS,
"The Deceptrices"

On her return to San Francisco in 1987, Lhasa asked her mother for singing lessons, and a professional coach was found. It wasn't the type of request Alexandra was likely to turn down under any circumstances, and Lhasa's artistic abilities were evident and far-reaching. She was an exceptionally talented portrait painter—with no instruction beyond a high school class, she produced surprisingly probing paintings and had a sophisticated sense of color picked up largely through an early love of Chagall and Van Gogh. She proved equally adept at any fine art she tried, including sculpting, collage, and crafts.

"Lhasa was an adolescent with a very old soul," says Ralph Dfouni. "Alexandra showed me videotapes from when she was fourteen or fifteen, and she was like she was when she was thirty-five."

That was far from the perception around the apartment, where Lhasa's proto-emo vibe often produced a roll of the eyes from her sisters.

"We were always super frustrated by Lhasa's way of doing things," says Miriam. "So shut down and contemplative. *Oh, my God, she's the most uninspired person on the planet! She's just sitting there! She doesn't do anything!* You'd want to shake her. She just sat around and hummed all the time and wrote poetry that was heartfelt and a little silly and over the top and kind of poor-me, woe-is-me, and we all thought, *Yech, . . . what is her problem?* Meanwhile, she's doing more than most."

Her sister, Samantha de la Vega says, "Every now and again I'd go home and Lhasa would let me use her room. I was pretty messed up at the time—I was looking for drugs and wasn't my highest self. Lhasa and I were similar in that we were kind of dramatic and both writing poetry from an early age. We would both write about death—Lhasa was going through this dramatic phase. It's funny: Ayin was the one who always wanted to go see *Purple Rain* over and over again."

At sixteen, Lhasa took her first very tentative public steps as a singer, performing at the Urban School, as well as at Café Fanari, a Greek coffee shop on Twenty-Fourth Avenue. Singing mostly jazz standards and tunes associated with Billie Holiday, she covered the material but gave no inkling of the depths she would explore just a few years later. "She sang in a high voice back then—it had yet to evolve into what it became," says Samantha. "I saw her at Café Fanari and it was decent, but it wasn't *oh, my God, that was so good*."

Lhasa spent her summers in Cabo, joining her father and stepmother and their three young children, Eden, Alex, and Ben (who use the surname Sela, rather than de Sela). As a result of Alejandro's teaching stint for the National Tourism Board, they had been able to acquire land at the tip end of Baja for next to nothing and build a small, rustic brick house with a thatched roof. "We went down to Mexico and ran a children's camp for a year-and-a-half, trying to make money," says Marybeth. "Lhasa came down for the summer and was one of our counselors. We did plays and songs and it was bilingual: Mexican kids and American kids singing in Spanish and English."

In 1990, Alejandro and Marybeth drove to San Francisco for Lhasa's high school graduation. Sky, who had left the Pickle Family Circus for a circus school in France and then worked with a small circus in Belgium, was also home. When she heard Lhasa was spending the summer in Mexico, she strapped her trapeze to the top of the Selas' van and joined them.

"We got there and Sky set up her trapeze in the lot next door to our house," says Marybeth. "And in those days there was nothing happening in Cabo, nothing going on here. So every afternoon at four, she'd do her trapeze act and Lhasa would sing a cappella in Spanish and English. In this empty lot. People heard about it and before long cars were pulling up at four, and people were setting up beach chairs. It was wonderful."

Though the de Selas had rarely been impressed by school curriculums—Miriam became a full-time circus performer at twelve and never attended an academic school again—Lhasa was eager to find a college program to enhance her readings and wound up at St. John's College in Santa Fe. Known for a unique curriculum built around an immersive reading of the "great books" and small seminar-style discussions—for example, a math class might read Pythagoras—it sounded like a good fit. It wasn't. She left after the first semester, uninterested in deconstructing and analyzing texts. Lhasa didn't want to conduct a postmortem on the bones and sinew of a story; she read to swim in their beauty and mystery. "She couldn't bear the way they taught," says Alexandra. "What she read needed to remain pure. Taking it apart interfered with the magic."

Unsure of her next move, Lhasa worked in a Santa Fe coffee shop and then opted to spend the summer of 1991 hanging out with her sisters. Following their previous summer in Mexico, Sky had submitted an audition tape and been accepted at Canada's renowned circus school, L'Ecole National de Cirque in Montreal, where Cirque du Soleil and others fish for new talent. Alone for the first year, she was soon raving to the others about the school and the city. "We all gravitated toward each other," Sky says. "As soon as one of us had a base somewhere, the others came—we had to be together. Ayin came and loved it and then Mama let Miriam come and live with her sisters. I think Lhasa came out of curiosity. Our basic thing as sisters has always been, *hey, come take a look at this*."

Quebec, settled by the French in 1608 and taken by the English in 1760, remains deeply French in culture. Life in Montreal is a tale of two cities: while approximately half of its residents are Anglophones, Montreal is also the second largest French-speaking city in the world. In the late 1950s and early 1960s, the province was riven by a French separatist movement that produced an exodus of many English-speaking residents—and major businesses—from Montreal to Toronto. Tempers had cooled considerably by the time Lhasa and her sisters arrived in Montreal and, somewhat ironically, the city stood on the cusp of an artistic and cultural rebirth largely because of its prior problems: its French personality made it the most European metropolis in North America and helped it to keep a commercial foot in Europe. This link led to vibrant businesses producing French-language films and music and French food, while the departure of so many English-speaking residents kept rents cheap. In the coming decades, the city would prove a hip haven for artists, musicians, filmmakers, and entrepreneurs, many of them opting for Montreal over more obvious choices like New York. Sophisticated and lively with room for growth, Montreal was unpredictable and refreshingly foreign at a fraction of the cost of Brooklyn.

But most of all, Lhasa and her sisters found the city liberating. "We had a very solemn and introverted childhood and adolescence and we *really* needed to party," says Sky. "Montreal gives an amazing opportunity: it's a safe place for a young woman to walk home at four in the morning—you can stay out dancing all night and nobody bugs you."

With both English- and French-speaking music communities, the Montreal club scene was unusually broad and inviting. A new friend Lhasa had met through Sky, Suzanne, suggested going to hear Térez Montcalm, a French jazz singer, at the Café Campus on Queen Mary Street. Still new to town, Lhasa spoke no French but was eager to learn about the music scene. At the show, she was introduced to another friend of Suzanne's, an outstanding guitarist named Yves Desrosiers. Lhasa was impressed that he played and recorded with singer Jean Leloup, a popular Quebecois rocker. With Suzanne acting as interpreter, she wondered what that was like. "Do people in the streets recognize you?" she asked.

As freeing as Montreal was, it didn't take the sisters much time to get down to business, especially Ayin, who had toured with the Pickle Family Circus as a tightrope walker. She had met and hooked up with Sotho, an actor and electric violinist, and they made an eye-catching pair. A tiny, sylph-like blonde with movie star good looks and a practiced poise drilled into her at a Guadalajara ballet academy, Ayin could have passed for Thumbelina. Sotho had hair down to his knees, thigh-high boots, and a broad dark smear of Goth eye makeup. During the summer tourist season, they took a portable six-foot-high wire into the streets of La Ville Montreal, the city's original quarter, and performed an arresting cabaret-class show. While Sotho played the violin, Ayin walked the wire and executed jumps and splits—first in toe shoes and then in high heels. For the show's capper, she balanced a ladder on the wire and—still in heels—climbed to the top. They performed as many as ten shows a day. Says Sky: "Everyone would gather around and they would make *lots* of money." They also became master entertainers: Ayin soon joined Cirque du Soleil and would later take what was essentially the same act around the world.

Eden Sela, then eight years old, didn't know what to think when she came up from Albany to visit her half-sisters. "Sotho was so, *so* out there—a Goth with platform boots and all this eye makeup! They were throwing a rave and Lhasa was sculpting a giant pterodactyl for it out of Styrofoam. She was really poor and had this crummy third-floor apartment somewhere in the Plateau with furniture she'd found in the garbage. Almost barren, just a mattress on the floor. She had a job at Les Foufounes Électriques, and she took me to work and made me a hot chocolate."[1] Eden's visit also coincided with Lhasa's newfound interest in hardcore music: she was sporting combat boots and a shaved head. It didn't last long. "She split her head open in a mosh pit and said, 'Okay, I'm done with that.'"

* * *

Lhasa didn't need a shaven head to make an impression. Her hair was just beginning to grow out again and she had a new job waitressing in a café and bar, the Mondiale, when a musician wheeling an upright bass down St. Laurent Boulevard stopped in and leaned his bass against the counter. "She didn't even ask me if I wanted a coffee," says Erik West-Millette. "'Who's your favorite bass player?'"

He rattled off his holy trinity—Charles Mingus, Jimmy Blanton, and Willie Dixon—and was surprised to discover she was more familiar with the jazz players than she was with Dixon, whose classic blues compositions—including "Spoonful," "Back Door Man," "You Shook Me," "I'm Ready," and "I Just Want to Make Love to You"—are deeply embedded in the pop and rock lexicon. "So I'm telling her that he played with Sister Rosetta Tharp and Muddy Waters and was also a great arranger and his mother, Mary Dixon, was a poet, and she's looking at me hard. I was kind of aiming for a coffee, but she said, 'Do you like Billie Holiday? Because I love Billie Holiday and want to do a tribute band.' I said I love Billie Holiday, too, especially the period with Lester Young, and we talked about songs like 'Solitude.' Very deep stuff for a young lady—like twenty, twenty-one. Finally, we had a coffee."

Sandra Khouri, a Montreal attorney who would become Lhasa's closest friend, was introduced to her at the Mondiale by a boyfriend. "She was already a very special creature," she says with a laugh. "She didn't have any hair and looked like a bully in a very fairy way. It was like, *who is that?* She had a rare and incredible beauty."

Their friendship began in earnest a few weeks later when, feeling alone and blue and aimlessly wandering the city, Sandra remembered the unusual waitress at the Mondiale and sought her out at the bar: "I was lost in the city and didn't know what to do. I said, 'Lhasa, I'm in trouble,' and she reserved a small table in the corner, put some candles on it, and just let me be there. And when she closed the bar the relationship began. We started talking and talking.

"What was great about Lhasa was that she was *so* conscious, so extremely conscious. Of everything. Of what was going on now. The people next to her. But she was not controlling at all. She would realize. I think this is the word she would say the most: realization. 'Sandra! We need to think realization! Think awareness of something.' That seeking awareness was constant.

"But, of course, I'm biased. I adored that person, that friend. We were really in love. If we were man and woman, I think we would have married. She was wonderful, absolutely wonderful. It was so easy for us to walk together."

Like Lhasa, Lousnak Abdalian had lived an unsettled, nomadic childhood. Her Armenian family had fled first to Lebanon and then traveled on to Paris and London before coming to Montreal. A painter, actress, and singer, she, like Sandra, felt both a deep bond and an instant conviction that Lhasa had a unique spark.

"Lhasa loved to write in cafes and there was one we used to hang around called Les Disparus (The Disappeared)," Lousnak says. "About two or three months after we met, I happened to walk in there and I wasn't expecting to see her and didn't even know she was there until she called my name. I don't know how to explain it to you except to say that no one had ever said my name like that. I can hear her now. There was so much in it: *Wow, I missed you! Wow, I'm so happy you came in!* All this in my name. And after that, we never separated."

Ryan Morey, who would later live with Lhasa and be her partner, saw an extraordinary complexity and span. "One of the unexpected things about Lhasa was that she was very down-to-earth and goofy," he says. "She laughed tremendously and often and had the most infectious laugh. She was an extremely dramatic and romantic woman through her twenties—the mischievous child and the ageless soul. There was a striking timelessness about her. How can someone be so goofy and deliberately ridiculous—and yet you know that you are with someone who is so conscious of the notion that you are connected, that it is your job to be part of the eternal and to manifest it? She's got both feet in that river."

The slowest nights for bars and clubs come early in the week, which is why many clubs are closed on Mondays, leaving Tuesday as the lightest night of the week. As a result, Lhasa didn't waitress on Tuesdays. Instead, she found bars that would let her sing a set a cappella. Wearing a black dress and a long knit hat, she cut a figure that was both striking and subdued.

"Lhasa had a unique way of dressing up," says Sandra. "She had a side that was very *pudique* (chaste, modest). She had a foot in the old world and a foot in the new world. She loved beautiful clothes, but you would not see Lhasa in a miniskirt and heels."

Working on the Billie Holiday songs and assorted standards, Lhasa was primarily focused on two tasks: overcoming her own shyness and learning how to hold a listener's attention. She had a ways to go.

"It was like torture to sit in the audience," says Sky. "Everyone was talking, and I knew she was thinking they would shut up. But they didn't immediately, and I sat there, suffering! She was giving her all. She sang with so much emotion, yet they kept on talking. So I left before she managed to shut them up. The next time I saw her was a few years later at the Bataclan in Paris—and I can tell you that no one talked!"[2]

But at that point, it was hard to see where Lhasa was going, if anywhere. Visiting his daughters, Alejandro was upset when he opened Lhasa's refrigerator and found only a small plastic pig that moved in circles and oinked when the door light came on; otherwise, the refrigerator was bare. He treated her to a parental shopping trip. And when she announced she was quitting her job, he delivered a fatherly sermon. "Lhasa, you don't have any food! You're behind in your rent. You have to work! Don't quit your job—you need that job."

Lhasa shook her head. "Papa, I'm a singer. If I can't sing—if I can't make my living singing—I don't want to live," she said.

The pragmatic and industrious Sky felt an older sister's dismay and disapproval. Fearful that Lhasa was being irrational and lazy, Sky wondered when she was going to stop hanging out in cafes and get a real job. "Which was a bunch of baloney," she says. "Actually, she was building it, leaning toward it. But you couldn't see it from the outside."

In fact, Lhasa was going through an intense period of absorption in which her skills as an autodidact served her well. After working in a small Quebec town for a few months, she returned to Montreal with a working command of conversational French. A self-starter for whom learning was synonymous with growth and growth synonymous with life, she needed no prompt to study. She sought to express herself as concisely and thoughtfully as possible— and not just in her music. She was also a devout letter writer and thought nothing of spending hours on a letter. More documents than casual missives, they might include ink sketches—a person, a place, a self-portrait—framed neatly by the text. Each was a finished work, and it is doubtful she mailed first drafts: no matter the language she wrote in, there was never a cross-out or revision. "My letters from Lhasa sustained me for years," says Sky.

Musically, her tastes were broad, but her system of learning was extremely simple and extremely focused. When she heard something in an artist or a recording that she wanted to emulate, she listened to the work incessantly for extended periods—sometimes months at a clip—until it was second nature. Particularly formative were some of the artists she had picked up on from her parents, such as the legendary cabaret star Chavela Vargas.

Costa Rican-born Vargas was a masterful singer of extraordinary depths who first rose to fame in the 1950s as a gender-bending nightclub star in Mexico City. It wasn't only that the hard-drinking Vargas dressed like a man, smoked cigars, and packed a gun, she also took possession of the *rancheras* traditionally performed by male singers while directing them to women. An intimate of Frida Kahlo and Diego Rivera, she befriended many of Mexico's leading songwriters and intellectuals, including the novelist Juan Rulfo, and later became a muse to the Spanish filmmaker Pedro Almodóvar and an international icon. She made her Carnegie Hall debut in 2003 at the age of eighty-three— two years after coming out publicly and proudly declaring she had never had sex with a man. Vargas continued to work and record—her aging voice singed by life but more moving than ever—almost up to her death ten years later. "I listened to those intense ballads all day, every day, for years!" Lhasa said.[3]

She developed a similar obsession with the Lebanese oud player and singer, Marcel Khalifé, an artist whose records

Alexandra had played. "There is a cassette that I have listened to hundreds of times—maybe thousands—and I know every single vocal inflection on that cassette," she told BBC reporter Stefan Christoff, stressing that it wasn't just about technique, but an attempt to connect with and intuit something of the ways that meaning and emotion were conveyed by an Arabic singer and "a little window into Arab culture." She found that the recordings of the Russian singer Vladimir Vysotsky likewise gave her some insight and an appreciation for that culture. "I don't speak Russian but I could just hear the humor, intelligence, rage and cleverness in Vysotsky's voice," she said. "This is the magic of music."[4]

Lhasa's musical tastes were largely defined by what she had heard her parents play in the bus, but her own earnestness would lead her to emulate the singers of deepest feeling: those capable of not only conveying the meaning of a song's lyrics but also crystallizing emotions beyond words. Likewise, her romanticism and spirituality led her to embrace singers such as Holiday and Vargas, whose music was inseparable from their tribulations, making them her artistic saints. The more she listened to and examined how a particular piece of music or performance made her feel, the surer she became of her personal aesthetics. "She was very opinionated," says Miriam. "She knew what she liked and didn't like. I remember many times going to see a show with Lhasa and she'd say, 'That was terrible, it was nothing.' To her it was very black and white. And that always impressed me. She knew *exactly* what she thought."

The next time she saw Yves Desrosiers, the guitarist with Jean Leloup, was at an outdoor café on Rue Saint-Denis. This time, she had the confidence to say she was a singer and to talk about what she liked. Writing his phone number on a matchbook, Yves suggested they get together and see what happened. "Maybe we can play in the subway or the street," he said.

Lhasa let a few weeks pass before phoning. In September, Yves came to her apartment with his guitar and a fake book,[5] and they tried a few standards. Listening to the way Lhasa sang, Yves wasn't sure what to make of her. It was obvious that she lacked experience, and despite taking her cue from Billie Holiday she didn't sound at all like a classic female jazz singer. "Her voice was somewhere else," he says. "Kind of androgynous, but strangely intriguing."

Looking for something else to try, he asked Lhasa if she liked bossa nova; she offered that she knew the Portuguese lyrics to a few Antônio Carlos Jobim songs. As soon as they started playing, Desrosiers could hear they were on a better track. "I felt something strong and smooth," he says. "And I told myself, *If this voice can reach me, it can reach a lot of people*."

As if to second that, Lhasa's neighbor stuck her head in the door. She and a friend had been sitting outside, sunning themselves and drinking wine. "Was that really *you* singing like that?" she asked.

By winter 1993, they had built a little repertoire, and Yves arranged a gig playing happy hour at a neighborhood bar he frequented. They performed mostly jazz standards and one or two Mexican *rancheras* that Lhasa had discovered through her parents' record collection. Yves was intrigued that this was a large part of the music she had listened to growing up. He liked the strange stories about her hippie childhood in the school bus and urged her to think about singing more songs in Spanish and fewer jazz standards. Aside from the fact that Lhasa sounded better singing them, Yves was convinced that it would make her stand out. "You really want to play that?" she asked guardedly. When he said he did, she was delighted.

With Lhasa pointing him toward specific records and performers, Yves began listening to more and more *rancheras* and other Latin recordings, and he bought a nylon-string guitar. The more they played, the more convinced Yves became that he and Lhasa were moving in the right direction. Erik West-Millette, the bassist who had met Lhasa at the Mondiale, was a close friend of Yves and they talked frequently about Lhasa. The guitarist was impressed by the surprising power and conviction she brought to the traditional Mexican songs and told Erik he saw an opportunity for her to develop a unique niche. There was no short-age of jazz singers on the Montreal club scene and this could be something different.

Though recording and working steadily with more established artists such as Leloup and the folk duo Gogh Van Go, Yves knew that he and Lhasa were onto some-thing. "I was busy working for bands and solo artists, but I was motived each time we played," Yves says. He also saw that Lhasa was green and that her enthusiasm out-stripped her experience. He wanted to boost her confidence by working as many gigs as possible. Over the next two years her French improved markedly—as did her ability to interact with audiences and tell stories between songs—and they began polishing a few ideas for demos in the small four-track "bedroom lab" Yves used as a home studio.

"She was damn lucky to meet Yves," says musician Pat-rick Watson, who was close with both Lhasa and Desro-siers. "The writing on that record is superb, and Yves is a really interesting guy; she ran into someone really caring. And also, like her, a bit out of this world. Similarly sensitive and reserved. It was a beautiful moment."

Yves and Lhasa spent long evenings talking about the kind of music they wanted to make and the elements they wanted to feature in the arrangements. Both were fans of the French band Bratsch, whose Gypsy music incorporates klezmer, jazz, North African, and other folk traditions. Yves pursued a similar eclectic approach in his arrange-ments, which Lhasa eagerly embraced: if the music's roots were largely Mexican, its leaves and branches were far more varied. Unable to play an instrument or write music, Lhasa conveyed her melodic ideas by singing, whistling, or humming, relying on Yves to flesh them out harmonically. Just as eager to develop Yves's ideas, she took recordings of several of his melodies home and wrote lyrics. Two songs grew out of this, "El Desierto" ("The Desert") and "El Pájaro" ("The Bird").

In 1994, one of their early demo tapes landed on the desk of Gina Brault, a Montreal radio programmer whose duties included booking performances for a live broadcast originating in a local bar. "A musician friend gave me a cassette with *Desrosiers* written on it and a phone number," she says. "I had no idea what was waiting for me." Indeed, though she loved the music and quickly arranged for them to appear on the show, Gina certainly didn't imagine she would become their manager—and Yves's wife.

With Yves as a musical partner and mentor, Lhasa was finding her lyrical and thematic inspiration in her ongoing conversations with her father. Even by the insular standards of their family, Lhasa and Alejandro had an unusually tight bond. "I have seven children, but Lhasa was unique," he says. "She was so intimately involved in those things that were close to me." And while Lhasa's sister, Samantha, describes both Ayin and their mother as more interested in spiritual practices than Lhasa—"She was not a pillow-sitter," Samantha says—it was Lhasa who gleaned the cultural and artistic implications from her parents' spiritual and mystical quest. Indeed, when she later told an interviewer that she "believes in everything—Buddha, Jesus Christ, Lau Tzu, astrology," it was easy to discern the hand of Alejandro. As wide-ranging as Lhasa's reading list was, many of the works she returned to again and again were the spiritual and theoretical texts that her parents favored, including *I Ching*, Paramahansa Yogananda's *Autobiography of a Yogi*, the teachings of Krishnamurti, and Carl Jung's *Memories, Dreams, Reflections*.

"Lhasa was interested in philosophical ideas regarding life and death and rebirth and spiritual consciousness," says Eden. "And so is my father. They had a connection because they were both obsessed with these ideas and would talk about them all the time. She was a very spiritual person but not in any formal or religious way—as a cosmic idea. Our father says he does everything, but when I read *Autobiography of a Yogi* as an adult, I realized that was really his core and what we were all raised with: these cosmic, mystical ideas about consciousness that are quasi-philosophical, quasi-spiritual, and quasi-scientific. It's hard to explain, but we were raised to perceive reality in a very interesting way. There was something literally psychedelic about our upbringing and the culture we were raised in. And it affected us."

Along with a streak of solemnity, Alejandro also shared with Lhasa a love of conversation. A gifted raconteur, he could be spellbinding while telling a story—a skill she would absorb and make a feature of her performances. "Her father had a great influence on her," says Yves. "They spoke the same language."

With Marybeth's encouragement, Alejandro had turned his Mexican forays as a language instructor into a career in upstate New York as a high school and college Spanish teacher. As Lhasa and Yves were crafting their first songs and demos, Alejandro was completing his dissertation at the University at Albany for a PhD in Spanish literature, with a focus on the literature of the Mexican conquest. "It was a huge topic, and he and Lhasa talked about it for hours and hours and hours," says Marybeth. "We would talk all night long," adds Alejandro.

Those conversations added greater depth and context to the way Lhasa thought about the *rancheras* that she and Yves had been performing. Just as key, her father's research and writing opened a new window on both the literature of Spain and the pre-Columbian Aztec poetry that, taken together, informed much of the subsequent Mexican culture.

One of the most well-known Mexican folk tales is the legend of La Llorona, variously translated as the weeping or wailing woman. Lhasa knew it as the mournful ballad recorded and popularized decades earlier by Chavela Vargas, and she sometimes performed the song in bars with Yves. But there are countless versions of the folk song, including some associated with the Mexican Revolution, and the legend that gave rise to them has just as many permutations and meanings. In perhaps its most well-known version, the legend tells the tragic and gruesome story of a woman betrayed by an unfaithful husband. In a fit of insanity, she punishes him by drowning their children; she is then doomed to wander eternally, crying after her children. Like American murder ballads, the folk tale served to castigate and caution women against giving in to their passions. Even today, a wailing Mexican wind is called *la llorona*.

Yet, as her father learned and shared with her, the story of La Llorona has an Aztec lineage as well, one that made the legendary woman far more prescient and heroic. In that version, she is a Native American Cassandra, appearing in a dream to warn of the arrival of the Spanish in 1519 and the coming conquest and enslavement of the people. "The Emperor of Mexico had a series of nine premonitions that his sorcerers said were alarming," says Alejandro. "One was of a rain of comets and another was of a wind blowing through Tenochtitlan and of a voice that could be heard in the wind—a woman's voice wailing, 'My children, my children, what will become of my children?' The sorcerers called her *La Llorona*, and Lhasa was very taken with that story when I told her."[6]

Inspired, she wrote the lyrics to what would become "De Cara a la Pared" ("Facing the Wall"), the opening song on her debut album, *La Llorona*. Based on an apocalyptic dream she had had of a city destroyed by fire and flood, it was a like-minded warning and a prayer for deliverance from suffering and hardship. Arranged on a lilting, airy violin theme by Yves, the album, like the ancient warning of La Llorona, seemed to float in on the breeze.

The ongoing conversations with Alejandro would provide the seeds for several songs, including "Los Peces," her take on one of Spain's oldest Christmas songs; "El Payande," a Colombian song from the 1870s; and "Por Eso Me Quedo" ("Why I Stay"), in the style of the great *ranchero* performer Cuco Sànchez. "La Celestina" is sung in the voice of a character from the Spanish play of the same name written by Fernando de Rojas in 1499, a tragicomic *Romeo and Juliet*. And with Alejandro she co-wrote the lyrics to "Floricanto," which echoed both the ecstatic poems of the sixteenth-century Spanish mystic St. John of the Cross and the traditional Mexican theme of the tragic nature of love and life. Though Lhasa listened to and loved music made by contemporary rockers—Tom Waits and Rage Against the Machine were particular favorites at the time—she had made an obvious decision to dig where no one else had. It wasn't a calculated decision.

"Her understanding of Mexican music was that it tended to be songs of broken-heartedness, of un-love and dislove," her father says: "Slavery: *my mother was a slave so I was a slave*. The lyrics to the song we wrote together have to do with mortality. I was reading Aztec poetry at the time and sharing it with her. That poetry was *all things are passing; don't be attached to life, we're all here for a short time, we all must die.* How the finest clothes turn to rags. This pessimistic strain in Aztec poetry carried on into Mexican folk music and cowboy songs that say, 'You're going to be sorry; I just laugh at the world because I know it's going to end, too.' Resignation to mortality is a predominant feature of Mexican culture and she picked up on that. And that vocal style that she was initially known for is the broken heart-break yodel born from that music. Like Billie Holiday, it is tragic and sad, and speaks of suffering, pain, and hardship. I think she was moved by that literature. It resonated with her."

Back in Montreal, Yves and Lhasa had expanded their performances to include the bassist Mario Légaré, accordionist Didier Dumouthier, and drummer François Lalonde. Like Yves, they were all experienced veterans of the Francophone recording and club scene and quick musical studies: wherever Yves and Lhasa took the songs, they could follow. Word of mouth was beginning to spread around town about the young Spanish singer with an unusual name and a good band, cemented by regular gigs at several bars including Les Bobards, Le Bar Barouf, and particularly Quai des Brumes, where Gina arranged a year-long contract for them to perform every other week. The work and strategy proved well timed: both the music and Lhasa's abilities as a performer were coming into much sharper focus. The same unusual level of awareness and thought that had immediately struck friends like Sandra and Lousnak in their conversations with Lhasa was now becoming just as apparent in her performances: on stage, Lhasa became intensely conscious of trying to make a connection with each and any listener. "Singing in the bars I learned how to reach people," she said. "Even people who were there just for beer and conversation."[7]

She was singing now with an intensity that, regardless of language, made for a riveting performance. "When I started singing and I got up on stage a lot of kind of unexpected things started coming out of me," Lhasa said. "There was a lot of sadness and a lot of rage. And those were the songs that I was attracted to singing. They were the songs that I felt the most when I was on stage."[8]

Guitarist Rick Haworth, a veteran of the Montreal music scene who toured extensively with Lhasa, says her onstage focus and commitment were extraordinary. "Lhasa had a work ethic that was brilliant and crazy," he says. "If she didn't bleed herself dry with every performance, she believed she was cheating the audience. She would dig deeper into a song than anyone I'd seen—she'd dig into the marrow of it. That was her challenge. I had to change the way I approached the songs—all of us did. It sounds touchy-feely, but she would get to a place in a song that was so emotionally advanced that if you didn't follow her you weren't part of the song anymore. You had to go there! Otherwise you're not doing it. There was no compromise: you had to bleed."

"Her shows were so personal and intimate," says Sandra Khouri. "She was extremely straightforward and kind of pure. In French we would say she was *sans fla-flas*—without pretensions. Absolutely none. It wasn't a show—you were going into her universe. She was a real magician of the soul."

Jamie O'Meara, editor of the Montreal entertainment magazine *The Hour*, had no idea who she was the first time he saw her. "She cut my then-girlfriend's hair," he recalled. "And this girlfriend dragged me out to Bar Barouf on Saint-Denis one cold January night to hear her haircutter sing." Wishing he was somewhere else and expecting nothing, O'Meara was stunned by what he heard—and by the audience's reaction. "It was, to say the least, transformative. I would see her again at the small pub Else's on Roi, and a handful of other quaint not-quite-venues where she was beginning to accrue a fiercely loyal following."[9]

One of those followers was Canadian music journalist Nicholas Jennings. It didn't bother him that Lhasa was singing in Spanish rather than French or English. In fact, it felt completely immaterial. "The language really did not make any difference," he says. "What she was putting across transcended language, she was such an intense performer. She had all the depth of emotion of an actress or an opera singer. You couldn't take your eyes off her."

The Montreal buzz that Gina had hoped for quickly materialized. A prime-time TV program on the Canadian Broadcasting Channel featured Lhasa and Yves dueting on a Mexican folk song. The next week the line at Quai des Brumes was down the block.

It didn't hurt that the local music scene had a vibrancy and fire that were both palpable and building. "Lhasa was coming out of a Montreal that was awesome," says Patrick Watson. "It was a magical moment—the kind you read about in a book and say, 'Fuck! I wish I was there!' My first show was in a porno theater. It was outside the 'stage' context so you were putting on an experience, not a show. People are there to have a good time. We used to play Café Sarajevo. They'd give you drinks and you'd sing on the tables. There was no business, no managers. We were completely sheltered from any idea of selling our music. One of the jokes is that French culture turned Montreal into an island. A lot of benefits came—it's one of the reasons we have good film directors—but business-wise, you're isolated and it's hard to get off the island. That meant someone like Lhasa or me or Godspeed You! Black Emperor were artistically free to avoid bullshit."

Moving from Yves's home recording setup to a small studio that François operated in a second-floor apartment between the Plateau and Chinatown on Saint-Denis, the guitarist and the drummer polished the backing tracks for Lhasa to add the vocals on a demo. When he and Lhasa were satisfied, Yves called Denis Wolff, an A&R executive at Montreal's Audiogram Records. Yves had worked with him on recordings for Jean Leloup and Gogh Van Go. Wolff, who had come to respect Yves and admire his work, liked the demo. And he liked what he saw from Lhasa in performance even more.

A leading French label, Audiogram had released a few records in English, but never in Spanish. No one was particularly concerned, though. "In Quebec, there's a strong tradition of liking world artists like Cesária Évora," Wolff says, and Audiogram had already had some success licensing and releasing an album in Italian by Paulo Conte. "These records did really well here, and we also have the jazz festival, which educated people. Plus Yves was involved with the local scene—some hip rock bands that had followings."

Continuing in François's studio, Lhasa concentrated on her vocals, but was loath to take even a small instrumental role. Says Desrosiers, "Lhasa was a bit intimidated back in those days about the recording process because she didn't play an instrument and I think she was afraid she would mess up my work. Even if I encouraged her to participate with easy things like raw metal percussions à la Tom Waits, she'd always decline." As a result, Yves became the music director of *La Llorona*, trading inspirations and melodic ideas with Lhasa and then building the arrangements and performances with François and the other musicians in the studio. "Lhasa was not present much," says François. "Yves and I would work on the music, and when it was ready, Lhasa would come in to sing or Yves would go to her house with a microphone." Several of the vocals recorded in her kitchen and initially intended to be used as guides proved good enough for the final record; a summer rain storm in Lhasa's backyard provided the album's opening sounds. "Yes, I was the architect of that record and sound," says Yves. "But Lhasa brought it to life. Without her voice and soul, we would not be talking today."

If the music and lyrics on *La Llorona* represented a unique and thoughtful exploration of a culture and tradition unknown to most listeners, the arrestingly colored yet stark painting she created for its cover dispelled any notion that this was a sociology project or a hip and obscure idea born of a clever ingénue's vanity. Rather, something intensely personal was at work. Lhasa used a mirror to paint what has been described as a self-portrait, but the piercing fiery eyes, hawk-like visage, and dark, somber facial tones are far more suggestive of her mother, Alexandra, with whom she had an unusually gnarled relationship.

Though Lhasa certainly loved her mother, she could not quite forgive her or forget the scenes that she associated with the splintering of the family. By comparison, her relationship with her father was easygoing and comfortable. She could not completely make peace with her mother—a painful situation that a now clean and sober Alexandra tried to accept with clarity.

"Lhasa was extremely critical of herself and of others," says Alexandra. "She was hard on herself—*really* hard on herself. Her journals are full of that. Endlessly. But she had plenty to say about others, too. We had some wonderful times and laughed a lot—her magnificent sense of humor saved her sometimes—but she couldn't be with me for long. It was almost as if she wished I was not quite who I am, wished I were different. You can't really do that."

Yet, whatever continuing frustrations and anger Lhasa may have felt toward Alexandra, the cover of *La Llorona* suggests that the album wasn't just paying tribute to a mythic mother wailing for her lost children. Lhasa didn't have to look across time to find a grief-stricken woman whose painful, self-destructive missteps had cost her her children. She had crisscrossed from Mexico to New York in cradle and car seat as that mother struggled to remake herself and regain her eldest daughters.

"Lhasa was alchemically able to take stories from our life that were tragic and turn them around and tell them in a way that would honor our family," says her sister Ayin. "She would talk about my father and honor him, talk about my mother and honor her. I think it was a self-healing tool for her to turn the pain into meaningful, soulful journeys that everyone can use as inspiration and hope and humor."

"When Lhasa was singing that darker thing—the way a fado singer would sing about the saddest life in the world—that comes from her mom," says Lhasa's friend Patrick Watson. "No mistake. That's her mother. The philosophy stories? That's her dad. But the shit where she opens her mouth and the world stops? Lhasa would be so fucking mad if she heard me say it, but that comes from her mom. I think Lhasa was singing the depth of her mother's experiences. She didn't experience them herself, but she saw the twists and turns."

Released in 1997, *La Llorona* garnered strong reviews, and Lhasa's following in Montreal and Quebec grew quickly. Its unique sound and tragic, passionate, romantic lyrics managed to both evoke an ancient mythic world and strike a timely resonance. Musician Thomas Hellman, who would become romantically involved with Lhasa some years later, was an undergraduate studying French literature at McGill University when *La Llorona* came out. "That album blew my mind," he said. "It came out in a dark and cynical time and on *La Llorona* she was able to embody romantic love and painful love at a time when that archetype was absent and sorely needed—it just didn't exist between people that much anymore."

BBC reviewer Malachy O'Neill said Lhasa sounded like nothing so much as an ancient matriarch and wondered how someone so young had conjured "heartbroken songs from a long life of exodus and lost love, offering ominous warnings of the weirder, darker corners of the human heart."[10]

"Almost right away there was success locally," says Denis Wolff. Several months after the album's release, Audiogram hired a publicist in Toronto and began publicizing the record in English-speaking Canada, a first step toward establishing Lhasa not just in the rest of Canada, but also in other English language markets, including the United States and the United Kingdom. Instead, events took a different turn: the stars were about to line up.

Shortly after the release of *La Llorona*, the band was invited to submit an application for a music competition. First prize was a trip to France and an appearance at the well-regarded Printemps de Bourges music festival. Neither Lhasa nor Yves liked the idea of playing in a competition, but Gina ignored them and put in the paperwork. A few months later, Lhasa and her band found themselves among the finalists performing at Montreal's Club Soda for an audience and a panel of judges. They came in first.

Excited by the opportunity to take a full band to France, they didn't quite understand what they had really won: Lhasa would be touted as the French-Canadian prizewinner at the festival's "Discoveries" series, one of the European music industry's most prestigious showcases. "I did not realize how much of a professional event this was, that it was not really for the public," says Gina. And once again, Lhasa was a hit. "After the performance, there was a line of industry people who wanted to meet Lhasa." Among them was Yves Beauvais from Atlantic Records in New York, who would release *La Llorona* in the States.

More important for Lhasa, however, would be her relationship with Tôt ou Tard, a savvy and well-run label that signed her for France. And they did so in no small measure at the urging of French music journalist Anne-Marie Paquotte, who had been impressed by her performance at Bourges. Then, in advance of Lhasa's Paris debut at the Bataclan, Paquotte wrote a glowing feature on her for *Télérama*, the country's most influential entertainment magazine. The result was instantaneous: overnight, Lhasa became a star in France.

Brazilian singer Bïa Krieger, who later became Lhasa's close friend, was living and working in France when *La Llorona* came out and Paquotte's article launched her. "Everybody was talking about her. *Have you heard this girl, Lhasa? Have you heard this record?* Getting an article in *Télérama* then was like having an article in *Rolling Stone* in 1968. Then everyone takes you seriously, everyone wants an interview. You couldn't go into a music shop without hearing her; her music was on the radio. Every festival I played at it was, *Do you know her?* I'm not a jealous person but you almost could be. Lhasa, Lhasa, Lhasa. It was huge. Huge."

Over the subsequent months, Lhasa and the band performed and built a following not just in France but also in Germany, Switzerland, and Belgium. Perhaps as important, her success in Europe would cement her reputation back home.

"A Spanish record made in Quebec?" asks Bïa. "Not a magic potion you would do again! But this reaction in France allowed a project that could have stayed local to become something else. When she got famous in France, she came back to Canada with a different status. She started out in Montreal as this girl who sang beautifully in Spanish. When she came back, she was a star."

— 3 —

THE PARADOX

In verse as in trapeze performance is all.

At home in Montreal, the success of *La Llorona* was explicit: worldwide sales of five hundred thousand copies and a raft of awards, including a gold record, a Juno—Canada's equivalent of a Grammy—for Best Global Artist, and Quebec's Felix Prize for World Music. But on the heels of her Canadian and European success, Lhasa would be stymied by a music market where her international success was largely meaningless. In the United States, listeners had no exposure to rock and pop artists singing in a foreign language nor any clue what to make of an American-born artist deciding to write and record in Spanish.

While Lhasa was making headlines overseas, one of the biggest music stories back home had been the 1997 debut of Lilith Fair. The all-women, multi-artist festival tour, founded by singer Sarah McLachlan, brought together such top performers as Joan Osborne, Tracy Chapman, Suzanne Vega, Sheryl Crow, and Emmylou Harris. And like many festivals, it featured second and third stages for up-and-coming and local performers. A Canadian, McLachlan welcomed Lhasa on the 1998 tour and spoke enthusiastically about her in interviews. For Lhasa, who up to this point had only gone from success to success as if in a dream, the festival would prove something of a rude awakening.

Virtually unknown in the United States, she was put on the second stage, where she found it difficult to connect with the audience. She was also proud and keenly sensitive about her status. Lhasa could tell herself that this was only her first real foray into the United States and that she had to put herself over, but it was painfully obvious that listeners and journalists had come for the stars they already knew and that her intimate style of performing—which relied so heavily on achieving a personal rapport with the audience to make the feelings behind the Spanish lyrics explicit—wasn't registering amid the hubbub of the tour. The *New York Times*, in a lengthy review of the all-day show, referred to her only in passing—and then as "the moody Spanish group Lhasa."[1] It was more than her pride could stand.

"It was very clear that there were biggies . . . the less biggies . . . the little ones . . . the real underlings," Lhasa recalled. While willing to take a share of the blame— "I was uncomfortable and I kept to myself and probably missed out because of that,"[2] she admitted—the experience clearly left a sour and lingering aftertaste. Though gratified to be given a comrade's welcome by the Indigo Girls and a bit starstruck when introduced to Sinead O'Connor, Lhasa would later roll her eyes and say she had no time for "whiny" female singer-songwriters: *Let's pick at the wound and see how much it hurts.* With all the self-analysis, people have forgotten how to tell stories."[3] And she was likely influenced by the indifferent reception she received on the package tour when she derided the mainstream music industry, calling it "Monsanto music—mass-produced crap that gives you a stomachache" and comparing its stultifying effect to the way in which genetically modified crops limit diversity in agriculture. Indeed, her festering anger and frustration were obvious. If this was the route to success, she didn't see herself taking that road. "Music illuminates the spaces available, the possibilities, encourages people to dream," she said. "Music can only maintain this role through maintaining its diversity. Musicians who don't allow themselves to be boxed in, or sucked in the money-making machine that is the corporate music industry, remind people that there are so many possibilities."[4]

Disappointed, she was unsure how to proceed. If artistically independent, Lhasa was also ambitious: if she was going to turn herself inside out on stage and in her songs, she wanted to be heard. She seemed, at least on the surface, completely at odds with the values and commercial rules of the music business. Did it really make sense to dedicate her life to touring and recording? Still, she found a measure of comfort and a bit of space in knowing that the critical, artistic, and financial success of *La Llorona* had at least earned her the time and freedom to set her own work pace and agenda and to seek answers to her questions. Her Canadian and French record companies, Audiogram and Tôt ou Tard, were already asking about her plans for a follow-up, urging her to work quickly rather than risk having her audience move on and forget her. It didn't strike her as a persuasive argument. If anything, she had been raised to constantly seek new directions.

"What was really passed to us in the way we were raised is that life is an interior search," says her sister Miriam. "A lot of soul-searching and trying to be truthful to your intuition. And in a very vague way trying to trust to something that's invisible. I would have to say that was a huge part of Lhasa's life: constant self-searching. I've thought about this so much—Lhasa's dormant periods were absolutely necessary for her to make her transformations."

While there was little Lhasa would have changed about *La Llorona*—she was pleased with and proud of it—she also had no desire to repeat it. It stood on its own, but didn't represent her own direct experiences. For all the emotion she had brought to it, her continuing artistic aspirations were starting to make her feel that it was life once removed: the work of a clever student and not a reflection of anything she had personally lived. She longed for a vibrant and conscious life—she worked at it daily—and viewed experience as the raw material of art.

"Her creative process was living and she didn't want to be known as a folkloric artist," says her friend Lousnak Abdalian. "The fact that the first album was all Spanish, it was very important for her to start coming out of that. We talked about it after *La Llorona* because the record company began to stress her a little to give them another one. And she didn't freak out, but said, 'I have to live. I can't write it unless I live it.' She kept diaries and had a lot of them. She wrote, wrote, wrote. She used to sing songs about bad love stories. And then she started living the stories and said, 'Oh, this is what I was singing about!' She didn't want that—she wanted to live life and *then* write about it."

In the end, Lhasa opted to make a radical move.

"I got paranoid," she admitted. "It seemed there was no room to live. I lost my sense of dignity."[5] She surprised Audiogram, as well as Yves and her musicians, with the news that she was literally running away to join the circus, leaving Montreal for France to join her sisters' troupe. As for when she was coming back, well, who could say? Maybe never.

For a young artist whose impressive first album and nascent career had been blessed with a measure of luck and a running start, it all had to seem inexplicable, as even she would later admit. "I look back and think it was a bit drastic,"

Lhasa said. "But when I left to go to France, it was almost like going to my death. I gave everything away. I did everything but shave my head and become a monk!"[6]

The idea was one that the four sisters had been discussing for a while. Sky—along with her husband, the Danish juggler Mads Rosenbeck, and their two young children—had been touring the world for several years with a small independent French troupe, Cirque Pocheros, the name a pun combining the French words for skin, flesh, and bone: *peau, chair, os*. Unlike an American circus, there were no animal acts, and the program was a good deal more theatrical and consciously artistic, but decidedly free-spirited.

"In France, circus is considered an art form," Sky says. "A lot of grants are given to artists and there's a system of festivals and subsidies. There's competition and pressure, but at least it's there—you can get support. And there was a wonderful revolution at that time in circus where it got more and more personal and creative, and the scene got punk and wild and different. There were other similar circuses but few enough of us that it still made an impression. Pocheros was not punk—it's almost impossible to describe, sort of a clay-and-bamboo experience—but it had its place and we had four very good years. We had a little money."

Within the family, Sky had always been something of a trailblazer. She went her own way—joining the Pickle Family in San Francisco, going to school in Montreal, settling in France—and Ayin and Miriam would invariably follow. "The four of us had an idea to do something together and I suggested that we do a Pocheros that would involve all of us together. That was when Lhasa interrupted her career. I realize now that what she did was extraordinary, but at the time I wasn't really aware of how successful she was. I didn't get what an amazing step she took out of a success and fame and into the mud that is necessary in circus life."

Mounting the show would prove an immense challenge. "We were kind of naïve and just hoping there would be a connection and magic would happen in a natural way," says Miriam. What it took was a lot of discussion, compromise, and work—not all of it easy or pleasant. Compounding the financial and physical challenges was the fact that as much as the sisters loved and were drawn to each other, their disagreements and sibling rivalry—especially between Ayin and Lhasa—could generate enough sparks to power a small town.

"We worked for months and there was a lot of disagreement, particularly regarding the name of the show," says Sky. "A lot of discord." Lhasa was dead set on calling the show *Cirque au Babel*—a sly commentary on how the four had competing visions of what the show should be and, as in the story of the Tower of Babel, couldn't speak a common language. "The others didn't want that," Sky says. "It was a really charged time."

Lhasa wouldn't back down. On January 6, 1999, the sisters marked Three Kings Day[7] by sharing a king cake—a tradition that includes hiding a jewel or trinket in the cake.

Whoever finds it is named king or queen and is granted a wish. When Lhasa found the prize, she held it up and pronounced her wish: "Cirque au Babel." Says Sky: "I remember thinking, *Ooooo, oh shit . . . I can't believe Lhasa did that—I would never dare.* But she meant it. She wanted to use her power in that moment to make something good creatively. And it was called *Cirque au Babel* at least for a while before it shifted to something else. It was a step in the process. You write the show as you improvise: you keep the things you like best, you weave it as the days go by, and out of these improvisations it becomes a living thing. You've got to be with people, but hold your own." That process wasn't just artistic. Along with Mads and the sisters, there were only two other performers in Pocheros. No director, no set designers, no laborers. It was just the seven of them to do everything, including building and acquiring props, setting up a tent, erecting bleachers to seat four hundred, and laying down a sand floor. "The first time we put up the bleachers, it took seven hours," Sky says. "We were all exhausted. But I remember Lhasa pounding in stakes and laughing. She liked it."

She also liked living a gypsy/carny life in a trailer. If that was run-of-the-mill for her sisters, for Lhasa, it felt far more romantic and satisfying than the hotels she and her band stayed in while on the road. On those tours, she had to drag along her own blankets just to make each strange room feel less impersonal; that wasn't necessary now. "It was amazing," she gushed. "My little niece would wake me up every morning by knocking on my caravan door and she would climb into my lap and say she loved me. If only touring could always be like that."[8]

Her friend, singer Bïa Krieger, thinks that was just the tonic Lhasa needed. "She had had a two-year touring period and was very, very lonely," she said. "She was touring with musicians who were all older, there weren't any other girls, and she missed her family. Also, I think she missed having time for herself. She would say, 'I played for a thousand people and they were adoring and then I went to my hotel room and was so lonely.' So she needed time and space."

Working out Lhasa's role was a bit tricky. "We came from the circus universe and Lhasa was like an alien," admits Miriam. "She was used to performing with good musicians and microphones and support systems and other things that had become natural for her to expect. And there was none of that. Instead, it was humid, and the sound was terrible, and we didn't know what to do with what she had to offer, and she didn't know what to do with what we were trying to offer her. But there were some magical moments."

The show that evolved was slow and contemplative: Ayin did her high-heeled high-wire act, and Miriam performed contortions on a ladder. Sky, who had retired from trapeze and had taken up clowning, flew above the ring in a strange boat outfitted with a wheel and a sail that was inspired by the paintings of the Spanish-born Mexican surrealist Remedios Varo. To accompany Sky's flight, Lhasa sang a new song written in French, "La Marée Haute" ("The High Tide"), backed by musicians playing accordion and guitar. She also sang a Mexican *ranchera* popularized by Chavela Vargas, "Luz de Luna" ("Moonlight"), and played rhythm games. The rest of the show included Mads juggling and talking to himself in Danish, as well as a performer who seemed to be eating his own brains.

"The spirit that came through in the end was luminous and intimate and a bit hard to define," says Sky. "A little animal and very feminine. And I think beautiful in the end even though we had a difficult time because of all the layers involved. It wasn't at all about impressing people with an act but about character and what happens between people. And not narratively driven. There's a thread you can follow, but it's furtive. Like a whisper. But from the inside it was very *chargé*—it had an electrical charge from all the people trying so hard to adapt to each other artistically and emotionally."

Creative and competitive issues simmered among the sisters as a matter of course. "Four sisters together," says Miriam. "There was a good chance we would kill each other!" But the biggest problem was their lack of funds: they operated on a shoestring budget without a crew. Bookings became sparse.

Cirque Pocheros fell apart dramatically almost a year to the day the project began. With a New Year's show to perform at La Seyne-sur-Mer in the south of France, the sisters had to drive their caravans overnight in a horrendous storm. "There were radio warnings against going out," says Sky. "I remember crying and saying to my husband, 'Why are we doing this? We don't have to die for circus!' I was so scared. And I dreamed that my trailer had blown away."

When they finally reached their destination, the weather was calm. Parking the trailers by the sea, they were advised to stay out of them that evening, as a waterfront fireworks show was planned. It proved a prescient caution: Sky and Mads's caravan was hit by falling debris and burned down to the wheels—a fiery exclamation point to the end of Cirque Pocheros.

"It was so apocalyptic," says Sky. "Lhasa later wrote a song about it, 'Para el Fine del Mundo o el Año Nuevo' ['For the End of the World or the New Year']. And there, in that same place, Ayin and Lhasa and Miriam all announced that they needed to not do this anymore. I was wrecked and didn't understand at the time that we were all exhausted and it was no longer possible. I just knew I had no home and my sisters were leaving. And that was devastating."

Still unsure of her path as a singer, Lhasa opted to stay in France, settling in nearby Marseille. Bïa Krieger had married Yves and Lhasa's friend, the bassist Erik West-Millette, and the couple were living nearby in Cassis. Lhasa bought a scooter and would frequently ride over to see them for long seaside walks, talking and trying to hash out what she wanted to do.

"She was almost overwhelmed by the success she had had," says Bïa. "Record companies don't want you to change your cloak because it complicates things. They were putting a label on her—she had this strong image as the Spanish-speaking son-of-the-circus girl—and that was only a part of who she was. She felt she was in a straitjacket: she had done this thing and now she wanted to do something else. She wanted to sing in English. Then she learned French and started to love French and write in French. So she needed time and space."

"When the circus was over, I spent a couple of years struggling to find a clear way to get back to music," Lhasa later said. "It wasn't simple. I was in Marseille because I didn't know where else I wanted to be and I didn't want to go back to Montreal. Marseille is a good place for people who don't know where they want to be."[9]

Particularly appealing was its diversity—both musically and ethnically. France's door to the Mediterranean and one of Europe's great waystations, the city draws people from all over the Middle East and Northern Africa: "the south of the north, the north of the south," as Lhasa would later dub the city in a song. Settling in, she was both eager to share her good fortune and to have people around who really knew her. Ayin had also settled there, and when Lhasa asked her friend Sandra to come from Montreal, they wound up spending a year together. Alexandra, who would ultimately live in Marseille for many years, also came at Lhasa's urging.

Lhasa's younger sister, Eden, visited a couple of times and spent a summer. She came away knowing two indisputable facts: the south of France was fantastic and Lhasa was the world's coolest big sister. "Marseille is an amazing city and she had a super-beautiful apartment," Eden says. "She was at the peak of her glamour in France and we had some wonderful times—she took me to an island on a friend's boat. I'm a fourteen-year-old girl from West Sand Lake, New York, and so my mind is blown. And she's like, *sure, you can smoke cigarettes! Go ahead, do whatever you want.*"

But Marseille also held a personal hook for Lhasa.

Her maternal great-grandfather, Basel Karam, had run away from his home in Lebanon as a child, stowing away in a boat bound for Marseille. According to family legend, Basel stayed in the French port city for a year before trying his luck first in South Africa and then Brazil. An adventurer, he was reputed to have joined revolutions wherever they occurred before eventually working his way north through Mexico to the United States. He became something of a talisman and ideal for Lhasa, and in later years, a large portrait of Basel hung prominently in her home. Inspired by his story—and seeing her own desires and wanderlust mirrored in him—she penned one of her first songs in French, "J'Arrive à la Ville" ("I Come to the City"), which she liked to introduce in concert by telling Basel's story as if it were a fairy tale with a mythical and moral tinge: "My great-grandfather was born in Lebanon, one of twelve children. He was the favorite of his mother. But his father detested him—and that posed lots of problems and instilled a fear in him. Basel learned to appear and disappear without noise so as not to be noticed by his father. But his father always noticed him and said his son was a bad spirit who haunted the house and caused all its problems and that it would be better if he disappeared for good. Basel used his gift of invisibility to hide in a boat bound for Marseille in 1895. He was eleven. He found work in the port, carrying bags and luggage. He never saw his mother again. One hundred years later, I went to Marseille and walked the same streets he walked. And I wrote this song for him." For Lhasa, walking those streets would prove transformative.

Bïa adored Lhasa. She also worried about her friend, whose sense of self and body image were punishingly harsh. "You would see her on the street and never look at her twice," says Bïa. "She was all crooked over and dressed in black. In Marseille, people are all tanned; it's like Los Angeles. Her hair was undone and her shoes were flat and big. I called her my little bird—she was like a bird whose feathers were wet."

Bïa's husband Erik was similarly flummoxed. "Her life was work, love, and her friends," he says. "But she had a lot of sadness—there was a lot of fighting in her family on both sides for generations and she was carrying a lot of that; everything was very tragic most of the time. I would say, 'Lhasa, homo sapiens aren't easy, but life is wonderful.' And she was super hard on herself."

A Louisianan for whom the existence of magic and spirits is a given, Erik always felt an unusually strong vibe from his friend. "Lhasa was seeing a lot of stuff—she had some kind of power. She was spiritual for real." Still, Erik was stunned when she said she was largely celibate and preferred platonic relationships. Puzzled by her reticence, he wondered if she didn't feel she was missing something in spurning sensuality. "She was into philosophy and research and said, 'No, if I can just talk, I like that better.'"

Part of it seemed a reaction to witnessing Alexandra's stormy outbursts when Lhasa was a child. While deeply focused on exploring her own feelings and beliefs, Lhasa always sought to be the master of her emotions, not their plaything.

"She didn't like emotional confrontations—it's one of the problems she had with me and her sisters," Alexandra says. "Lhasa was much calmer and much less emotionally expressive than the other three or me. I know I drove her crazy and I think her sisters did, too, and she adored them. It bothered her; she thought we were all drama queens. We weren't. We expressed things differently from the way she did. But her journals are full of all that she felt and suffered—I mean, just full of it. But she didn't express it outwardly the way they did or the way I have."

The harpist Sarah Pagé worked with both Lhasa and Ayin, befriending each. "In Ayin, I see all the emotion and intensity of Alexandra that Lhasa didn't want anything to do with," she says. "Ayin and Lhasa butted heads because Ayin is proud of being emotional. She just relishes it."

If fearful of becoming an emotional mess, Lhasa was nevertheless always a true and unabashed romantic. There were several years when her approach to love bordered on the monastic—a reflection of the intense self-examination, brooding, and desire for perfection she had picked up from her father. She told friends that she was working to prepare herself in all aspects for the man she was sure she was destined to meet—and had faith that he was preparing himself for her. "She idealized love. She really believed she was going to meet the person meant for her," says her friend Lousnak.

"She couldn't speak about love from knowledge," says Bïa "She was dreamy and would fantasize about ideal men, but she wouldn't touch them; only in her head. I've known guys to say 'I was her first boyfriend.' No. Maybe they thought they were. She may hang out with them, but her dreams were elsewhere."

None of which prevented her from going out with men, or cutting loose—sometimes in spectacular style. A strict vegetarian, she liked to dance and to drink whisky and tequila, and she was an avid cigarette smoker. "She was so funny," Erik says. Indeed, her sexual reserve notwithstanding, she loved dirty jokes and told them better than anyone in their circle. "If there was a dirty joke contest, she won all the time," he says, recalling one night in France when, following a broadcast appearance, the musicians stayed up all night in the hotel drinking brandy, and Lhasa, "cracking the nastiest jokes," drank everyone under the table. "She was always bumming cigars off me," he says, remembering another night—this time in Lafayette, Louisiana—when Lhasa kept the room laughing with a continuous cascade of jokes, some of them exceedingly dark.

"The paradox of Lhasa," Erik says. "She was a powerful woman and a little girl at the same time. Two sides in confrontation."

The only place it could all be expressed at once was onstage.

She had been keeping a low profile in Marseille, living anonymously. But when a group of circus performers that Lhasa had befriended came through the city, she agreed to help them drum up business by performing with their pianist in the tent they had pitched in a park. She showed up in her usual black dress and flat shoes.

"She was dressed like that with her hair up in an ugly bun," says Bïa. "And she started to sing with her eyes closed and would not look at the people, was not making any gestures, and all the noisy people fell silent. It was incredible. It just happened. In that flea circus! Outdoors of Marseille, nothing there. The lights were ugly, the sound was shitty, people standing up on sand, and she was there in those horrible shoes, and you couldn't ever, *ever* have an uglier hairdo. But she was magnetic."

In conversation, her sense of humor could be disarmingly light, even childish. "Where does Napoleon hide his armies?" she would ask friends with a giggle. "Up his sleevies!" Yet, something sad and angry and deeply considered would bubble to the surface when she sang.

David-Etiene Savoie, who met Lhasa in Marseille and later became her road manager, was not surprised by the transformation she underwent the minute she stepped into the spotlight. "A lot of singers are like that," he says: "You see them onstage and in life and it's such a different world. But one thing that amazed me was that it seemed easy for her—some people need to say, 'Okay, I'm going into that zone' and meditate for an hour and she did not. A minute before going onstage she could be very silly, making jokes, and then it's, 'Okay, Lhasa, you need to be onstage,' and she would switch and become that. And it seemed easy for her. It was not acting—it was sincere and she could go from one extreme to another. Because it was something more personal than acting. All those things were in her and she knew those different parts. They didn't need to be called forward."

Even her sisters could be surprised. "It wasn't like Lhasa was any deeper than anyone else in the family," says Samantha. "I went to see her once in Vancouver and a seventy-year-old woman turned to me and said, 'Oh! How can someone so young be so profound?' And my first thought was, *Oh, man, I'm gonna puke*. It seemed so silly at the time because it's Lhasa, you know? And she's saying shit I've been hearing my whole life from Ayin, from Sky, Miriam, and Gabby, from my mother and stepdad, *everybody*! Lhasa would get offstage and be quiet and withdrawn. It took a lot for her to confront the world. Yet, when it came to actually being herself, she was unequivocal, and there was no other way it could be. And I saw that her performance was where she was able to be her most wondrous, realized self. She really showed up onstage and in the most gentle, delicate, tender, powerful way. And sang with a slowness that made her even more vulnerable—it takes courage to be slow. She focused it all in her art."

Among those struck by Lhasa's impromptu performance in the park was a young music student who had played a bit of circus music. Jerome Lapierre, like Lhasa, had only recently come to Marseille, and he was able to wrangle an introduction. They hit it off and started to see more and more of each other, and he eventually moved in with her.

"She spent a lot of her time writing," Jerome says. "She took a lot of time to live and think. She had the pressure to produce a second album, and I think she fought it well. It was too much too fast, and she managed to escape from all that bullshit. She needed to spend some time in the mud and not fight life."

Audiogram executive Denis Wolff was dispatched to Marseille to get a read on the situation. "There was a distance all of a sudden. Yves had a hard time. I think she resented—although maybe that's not the right word, maybe she was frustrated—that she couldn't play an instrument. She would hear music in her head and felt a bit dependent because Yves did all the music. She had good taste and was very well read and wanted to realize her own vision without completely knowing how or what. And she was also very much in love with Jerome."

Along with her constant reading, music, of course, was her lingua franca. Lhasa and Jerome listened intensely to an unusually broad range of recordings: she particularly liked Radiohead, Tom Waits, Beastie Boys, and Beck and was going through something of a hate phase in her lifelong love-hate relationship with Bob Dylan. "She would get really angry about Dylan sometimes," Jerome says, "and say he was too cynical. For her, it was always important that people never give up." But along with rock were great international singers of deep feeling, like Lebanese diva Fairuz and Egypt's Oum Kalthoum, as well as a steady diet of Portuguese fado and classic flamenco recordings.

Her reverence for the power of music to shatter boundaries became apparent to David-Etiene Savoie when he approached her about appearing in a show in Paris organized by a troupe of Chechen dancers stranded in France by the second war in Chechnya. "The idea was to invite singers to perform Chechen songs, record them, and send them to Chechnya because their culture was so torn down by the Russians," he says. "We thought having songs by foreigners singing in Chechen would have an impact on the population." Unsure how Lhasa would respond—9/11 was still a fresh catastrophe, and the Russians had branded the Islamic Chechens as terrorists—he asked her to come and sing.

"This is one of the things I want to do with my music," she said after David explained the project and its potential PR pitfalls. "This is what music is for."

The biggest hurdle was the language: Chechen is difficult to pronounce, and the artists in Paris were working with a language coach. Alone in Marseille, Lhasa had only a sketchy-sounding cassette of the song she had selected and was obliged to learn it on her own phonetically. As if that wasn't weighty enough, the song, which translates as "A Last Prayer for My Friend," has the deepest emotional resonance for Chechens.

"When a Chechen dies, their body has to come home," David explains. "It's super important to be buried in Chechen soil. A lot of young men disappeared during the wars and the Russian army essentially kidnapped the bodies and ransomed them back to the families for burial. That's what the song was about—about coming home to be buried—and it was a very important song for the community."

Lhasa mastered the song on her own by ear. Indeed, her performance and recording proved the show's only unequivocal success. "The Chechens were very touched," David says, "but they said, 'We can't understand a lot of it. Except that one singer who didn't have a coach.' A photographer friend who was instrumental in organizing the project later showed me a picture of a Chechen man crying while listening to Lhasa's song. And my friend said, 'To make a Chechen man cry, you have to wake up early. I never saw that before.'"

Once again, the high standards and seriousness that Lhasa brought to her work had set her apart, showing that her keen focus, her unyielding faith in the romantic and the mystical, and a stubborn, hyper-critical nature were strengths in her career. But those attributes, that focus and intensity, did not work as well in her life beyond music.

"It was so clear to me that her albums were very much her babies," says her sister Miriam. "She needed that space to create and, in my opinion, there's no way she could have shared that with a child at that time—and she adored my two boys. At the end of her life, children were something that she really, really wanted. But at that time in her career, it seemed perfectly normal and right that she did not have children or a family. That was definitely pushed to the side. I don't think she could have had a husband."

Yet, if living was the wellspring she required for her work, Marseille and its diversity had proven a good choice, allowing her to refresh herself and explore new directions. With an expansive command of French and the confidence earned with *La Llorona*, she was now writing songs in Spanish, French, and English. And she had a strongly defined sense of which language best suited the emotions or ideas she sought to put across in each song. "There's a difference in her writing in the different languages," says Bïa. "The French is more synthetic and the Spanish more dreamy—images like you might find in Gabriel García Márquez. In English, you can see the influence of Bob Dylan or Leonard Cohen. What she's writing in English is often complicated and very philosophical: life and death and being born."

Lhasa wrote daily, making extensive use of notebooks. She found this the best way to turn her personal experiences and feelings first into shareable ideas and then into songs. She had likely discovered and adopted the practice from the work of Theodore Roethke, one of her mother's favorite poets and a fanatical notebook writer. Roethke believed personal life and experiences to be the only trustworthy source for poetry and that notebooks were the best way for a poet to capture and distill images and lines out of those experiences. It was a method he lectured and wrote about for several decades as a professor of poetry and one that Lhasa came to share. *La Llorona* now felt at odds with that.

"When I did the second album, I was trying to do something intimate and personal," she told journalist Madonna Hamel. "It was in three languages and I was a little bit nervous about it. I am just barely brave enough to do [my albums]. And then when I do, the road just opens up and I think, *why was I so afraid?* Even me, brought up the way I was."[10]

At the heart of her search for something "intimate and personal" was a desire to use music to convey her faith that life has a larger cosmic sense and purpose that transcends the individual, even if she couldn't always perceive it. Likewise, she felt deeply that life has meaningful spiritual and mystical components that can be experienced and conveyed through art even if never explicitly expressed. Lhasa believed in synchronicity. She characterized truth as elusive and hard to pin down, "something you glimpse only sometimes from the corner of your eye,"[11] and felt her work came closest to it when brushing up against and evoking the inexpressible. The stories that affected her most deeply were archetypal and allusive rather than concrete. "Fairy tales, mysticism, and romanticism were really the three parts of her recipe," Eden says.

Like her parents, Lhasa employed the *I Ching*, an ancient Chinese system of divination that, in modern usage, relies on calculations based on tosses of coins (the original technique used yarrow stalks) to answer questions. After tossing the coins—or "throwing the *I Ching*"—the resulting symbol (a series of six lines) corresponds to a paragraph in the book indicating what path to take. Searching for portents and symbols, she consulted yarrow sticks and tarot cards and had her own personal rituals.

"It comes down to searching for answers to the unanswerable questions," says Alexandra. "The *I Ching* is like the Bible: you can find anything you want in it. Lhasa had an unending quest toward those questions that have no answers, the life and death, art and love questions. When she was sick: *why*? Who can answer that? *I Ching*, tarot were just helpers to try and find the answers to those questions. And those answers were never really found, but she needed to continue to search for answers to the impossible questions. It wasn't a casual, amusing thing. It was the center of her life."

That search for symbols and signs also included a raft of daily routines, games, and superstitions. "When Lhasa and I lived together in Montreal, we had endless rituals," Miriam says. "We also had an ongoing joke: *houses are for spaces*. Lhasa liked to create spaces all over the house where you wouldn't put anything, and it was important to her—it was her version of feng shui—to make these respected spaces. And every morning we would get up and play scorpion—it was our ritual. We would play solitary, but together. That was Lhasa: we didn't play a game together, but we played side by side every single morning. And if we won the first game that meant the day was going to be absolutely exceptional. If we won on the second game, it was going to be good. And if we won on the third, it wasn't going to be that great. If we didn't win at all, we might as well just go back to bed."[12]

Perhaps even more important for seeking insight from the inarticulate and unconscious were dreams. She used her notebooks to distill those fleeting glimpses into words and stories.

"Lhasa was an incredibly vivid dreamer," says Miriam. "She dreamed in lucid images—very symbolic and beautiful—that she could always remember." To help unravel those images and impressions, she became a devoted reader and follower of the psychiatrist and philosopher Carl Jung, whose theories on the collective unconscious and universal archetypes captivated her. Reading Jung, Lhasa became convinced that her dreams provided a window into images and desires common to everyone—and that she could mine them for allegories and songs that listeners would recognize as their own deep yearnings.

"I think that dreams are our soul speaking to us," she told the BBC. "It's a part of ourselves that we don't know very well. The psychologists call it the 'unconscious,' but I don't really like that word because I don't think it is unconscious. I think it's extremely conscious. It's just that we don't touch it very often. Dreams are your soul forcing you in some way to make that contact, and it's up to you whether you pay any attention or not."[13]

While allowing that some dreams are meaningless, Lhasa considered other dreams life changing and deeply philosophic. In one, Lhasa dreamed she and a sister were living a life of drugged torpor in a basement apartment. Though the space had a pool in the middle and at first felt cozy, it soon became obvious that it was a cell in a prison. Every day the cell would get progressively hotter and the sisters would have to take refuge in the pool, staying underwater as long as possible while everything around them burned. The room would then slowly cool and they would emerge from the water into comfort, only to have the cycle repeated day after day until Lhasa convinced her sister that they must escape. After hours spent loading a wagon, they traversed a courtyard where soldiers with machine guns stood guard on the walls. First fearing they would be shot, she intuited the guns were a bluff and that the sentries relied on the prisoners' fear. Indeed, the dream ended with the sisters walking through the gates unmolested and into the freedom of nearby mountains. Upon awaking she had been struck by the dream's simplicity: the open-door prison that relies on chains of lassitude and inertia. It was an obvious and useful metaphor regarding the tendency to drift unquestioning through life, accepting limits and conditions and being complicit in one's own jailing. "The guards, who are just like scarecrows, don't have any real power," she said. "That dream made me realize that freedom is just having the courage to live your own life."[14]

— 4 —

MILE END

What I learned from Buddhism was that
I did not have to know myself analytically as much as
I had to tolerate not knowing.

MARK EPSTEIN,
Going to Pieces without Falling Apart

If dropping off the map and settling in Marseille had seemed puzzling and risky moves, Lhasa, after nearly three years in France, now held the payoff: interspersed among the sketches, observations, ruminations, self-recriminations, and fragments of dreams that populated her stack of notebooks were numerous songs—including a dozen she felt were ready to be recorded. Unlike *La Llorona*, the new songs grew out of her own peripatetic existence and longings. They were songs of desire, bitterness, pleasure, spiritual yearning, doubt, and surrender. Lhasa may have kept a tight rein on her relationships with men, but she clearly could dream up a storm: two of the new songs, "Pa' Llegar a tu Lado" ("To Reach Your Side") and "Con Toda Palabra" ("With Every Word"), were intensely passionate and romantic, with intimate physical images of being overcome and subsumed by love.

"Some writers don't have to live every situation to understand and write it," says her friend, Ralph Dfouni, who directed the video for "Con Toda Palabra." "It's a blend of sensitivity, intense observation, and some natural talent: you can write a situation in a truer way than somebody who has lived it. If she had not lived in particularities like love, she had lived in other ways and could transpose her conditions and understanding and anguish into these spheres she hadn't yet lived. She was very good that way."

While Lhasa's art may have come down to grappling between the opposing bookends of her mother's passions and anger and her father's austere and prideful quest for a life of enlightenment, she nevertheless craved independence from both. In a couplet written for what would prove her next album's keystone track, a chronicle of her own wanderlust titled "Anywhere on This Road," Lhasa stood firmly between those two poles and discovered her personal mantra: *If I can stand up to angels and men / I'll never be swallowed in darkness again.*[1]

Alejandro had been her partner and guide for much of *La Llorona*, yet her new work both stood on its own and questioned some of his assumptions. It was Lhasa's strength and curse to weigh everything and everyone and even her father was not immune. "La Confession" is filled with the kind of brutal self-criticisms that kept Lhasa's mother worrying about her; it also longs to be free of the lofty expectations instilled by Alejandro.

To find musicians, Lhasa turned for advice to her friend Arthur Higelin, a Parisian musician, singer, and composer who performs as Arthur H. He introduced her to a group of musicians in Paris, led by the cellist Vincent Ségal, who he felt would be right for her. It quickly became apparent, however, that the match wasn't working—through no fault of the musicians.

In Montreal, Yves Desrosiers had developed an intimate knowledge of her tastes and strengths, so it didn't matter that Lhasa couldn't read music and knew virtually nothing about formal composition or harmony. "She's a genius, but for the first ten years of her career, she didn't have the skills, technique, or vocabulary," says Bïa. "She would sing the melody and expect the chords to be played. That's the magical chemistry that happened with Yves. He could guess what she was expecting to hear and they made that extraordinary record. In Paris, she wasn't able to boss the musicians around or at least direct them. She couldn't say, 'Guys, this is what I want.' She needed perceptive, intuitive, sensitive people. And the musicians in Paris were not that kind of people. 'You want it another way? Show us or we're going to tell you what's good for you.' I saw her when she came back from those sessions and she was perplexed. She didn't say, 'They do minor when I do major,' just 'The magic is not happening.' And with Lhasa, everything was about the magic." If Lhasa was really ready to record, Bïa suggested, then she ought to consider returning to Montreal. "That's where the people understand you," she said. "That's where your mojo is. Go see Yves."

Leaving Jerome was not an easy decision. "I thought she would stay in Marseille," he says. "But that second album was impossible to do in France and she said, 'I have to leave.'"

Yet, when Lhasa got back to Montreal and showed Yves the songs she had written, saying that she wanted to expand the music in other directions and add lyrics in English and French, he was skeptical and flatly said that her new material didn't move him. The implication was clear: why mess with something that worked? They agreed to continue talking, with Lhasa saying she would start working in the meantime with François Lalonde, who had been Yves's co-producer on *La Llorona*, and pianist Jean Massicotte.

Lhasa and Yves never worked together again. Whether it was Lhasa's need to follow her own artistic vision or Yves's pride in guiding the compositions as musical director, each had a different view of what had gone wrong and who was to blame. "It's like a couple," says Bïa. "*Who left who?* I don't think you can say she left him at all. They left each other."

"We still talked sometimes after that, but things weren't the same," says Yves. "With time, I've realized that I'm not an easy person to work with. Lhasa and I were both painters and a painter is a loner. I was something like a mentor and it was time for her to make things by herself. And she did great after *La Llorona*."

"We were all surprised when Yves wasn't involved in that second album—the first one was perfect," says guitarist Rick Haworth. "Yves had worked with her so closely and so well. And yet, she was going to give that up to go where she had to go. She had that clarity."

"I think in your late twenties you start to learn that there is a choice that you have to make," Lhasa said. "Either you go your own way or you go other peoples' way. And if you go your own way, you have to start listening to yourself and trusting yourself. . . . So the whole album was written in a period when I was starting to push back. . . . It has the feeling of reaching a turning point where I am going to make choices from now on. I am not going to betray myself."[2]

On the verge of turning thirty, Lhasa had already walked away from a romance with Jerome in Marseille and a partnership with Yves in Montreal when they proved a hindrance to her work and will. Still, it was hard not to wonder what part Lhasa's upbringing played in her ability to jettison even the closest friend or collaborator. As a child, she'd never had a home that lasted long, never had a relationship outside her immediate family that hadn't proven transient. And even as an adult with a wide circle of friends, she would prove to be a loner, reliant only on her own internal voice. "She kind of fit in everywhere but also nowhere," says her half-brother, Mischa Karam. "And that's also the way the family is and the way she was raised. There's an internal thing where you don't ever feel rooted in yourself and there's constant movement; things are never settled. There's a beautiful part of that, an openness to the many different things you see and experience and touch. But there's also a lot of wondering *what am I doing?* And I think that's a family trait."

Yet, slowly and thoughtfully she had come into her own as an artist. The years in Marseille had provided the time and distance to re-examine not just her work and goals but also her assumptions about life. Following the release of *La Llorona*, her father had sent her a book, *Del sentimiento trágico de la vida* (*Tragic Sense of Life*), by the Spanish philosopher Miguel de Unamuno. It had precipitated a crisis in the young singer. She would later joke in concert about the doubts it had produced, while telling a tale laced with magical realism.

"I think the book was written primarily to make people have a deep existential crisis," she said. "And I think my father sent it to me because he thought I was ready for one. So I read it and it worked perfectly. And I immediately fell into a deep, deep, deep hole. And I was crying, thinking about life all the time, walking down the street and looking at people and wondering how they could pretend that things were normal. This went on for months and months. Finally, I went out in my back yard and sat down and was feeling very tragic and depressed, all wrapped up in thoughts. All of a sudden, two black birds flew onto my shoulders—this is a true story!—and they started screaming into my ears. And they screamed so loudly that I got scared and ran into my apartment. And the birds came flying in after me! I chased them out and slammed the door and then they came in through the window. I chased them out again and closed the window and they sat there outside my window all day long. Just staring at me. And I sat down and tried to go back to my tragic thoughts because I'd been doing it for a long time and really didn't know what else to do at that point. But I couldn't do it anymore. I felt those birds had come to wake me up and to say that that was enough of that and it was time to start living life without having any answers."

Living life without having any answers. Conveying complex, deeply examined points of view with a childlike purity was emerging as a defining characteristic of Lhasa's work. The paradox at the center of her personality—a sophisticate's deep enduring melancholy and an innocent's equally ceaseless wonder and faith in magic—would be evident in the lyrics and music of her next album: Edith Piaf crossed with Tinkerbell.

"That world of fairy tales that she grew up with—it didn't fade away with Lhasa as with most people," says her road manager, David-Etienne Savoie. "She gave me the uncensored version of *Tales from the Thousand and One Nights* and said, 'You need to read this to understand the real shit about fairy tales.' It's very violent and intense, very bloody, but she loved those. For her, it wasn't about being cute but about being in resonance. Life is amazing but not cute."

"She had an insane integrity," says Miriam. "She was perhaps the most integral person I ever met—completely true to herself. That sureness was something I think she created. She decided at one point, *I know. If I just lean in and listen I'll get clear information.* And once she decided that, oh boy! And the more she did it, the clearer it got. It was something she practiced. It was part of the work she did—to become *extremely* clear about her opinions and desires, what was fine work and what was not."

Masterkut, Jean Massicotte's studio on Boulevard St.-Laurent in the Mile End neighborhood, became Lhasa's workshop. Meeting every day, Lhasa, Jean, and François didn't jump into recording so much as ease into it, searching for the right feeling. She told them that she wanted the record to feel "inexorable"—a word that she repeated so often that it became something of a joke among them. But it was clear from the lyrics what she was after, a sense of life as an unstoppable, ever-turning wheel. Says Jean: "It was never about trying to match that kind of music or this one. We would have long conversations about life, politics, music we were listening to, movies, books we read as kids. She had a very, very strong spirit, a lot of certitudes and a very penetrating take on things. She didn't have many doubts, particularly about music." The pattern continued even as they began recording: the musicians would wander in and chat for an hour or two before going into the studio for sessions of between two and five hours. "It was a very relaxed way of working. Always daytime, never evening," says Jean.

The album took a year to complete to her satisfaction, but it rarely felt unmanageable. "Lhasa was easy to work with," says François. "We took our time and concentrated deeply on the mood, song by song. Sometimes Lhasa would say, 'I don't really like this.' Okay, we'll search for something else. But she was marvelous—like sunshine."

At first, it was just the three of them: Lhasa would bring in a melody, and it would be up to the drummer and pianist to work with her to find the chords and arrangement appropriate for the mood she wanted to convey. It was largely a process of trial and error, with Jean and François presenting a variety of voicings until the music matched what Lhasa was hearing in her head. "She would come sit at my side on the piano bench," Jean says. "She would sing, and I would start super slowly because I knew if I started with chords she'd say, 'No, no, stay closer to what I'm doing.' She couldn't say, 'Play a diminished chord here.' Or, 'Play this minor seventh.' She didn't have the vocabulary. But she was a musician; she just didn't play an instrument."

Her most insistent instruction was simplicity: an arrangement had to underscore and amplify the melody, not embroider it; every change had to develop rather than obscure a song's initial inspiration. "She was very good at focusing on that," says Jean. "Whatever we add should reflect what is already there."

It proved a uniquely personal and intuitive way of collaborating—one in which the collaborators almost had to take Lhasa into their heads—as became apparent to Massicotte when he awoke one morning to realize he had been dreaming the piano part on "Pa' Llegar a tu Lado" to pair with her intimate, breathy, delicate vocal. "The whole night I could see my hands on the keyboard playing the same thing over and over again," says Jean. "I came to the studio and said, 'We have to record 'Pa Llegar' today! I know exactly how it should go!' And she heard it and said, 'That's it! Don't change anything.' So when I say we didn't do a lot, it's in that regard."

The music emerging didn't so much break with *La Llorona* as take its motifs and expand and modernize them. The first album, with its Spanish lyrics, folk tunes, and old legends, was a musical séance conjuring the spirit of another era. Now those same timeless verities—the search for love, meaning, and self—were placed in a broader contemporary context, the voice and stories far more recognizable and personal. It was perhaps the first album in three decades—since Joni Mitchell's 1976 landmark *Hejira*—to map the odyssey of a woman simultaneously scouring the landscape for her reflection and her soul for a vision of the world.

Like *La Llorona*, the new collection was proving decidedly exotic, its French, Spanish, and English lyrics forcing most listeners to get out of their comfort zone and work a little harder, to listen and look in different and unfamiliar places. The same was true of the music, which had an international feel—not surprising considering Lhasa's listening habits and the album's origins in the diaries of a Mediterranean journey. Where Lhasa and Yves had reached back in time for the music of *La Llorona*, she and her musicians now stood firmly in the present, using modern studio techniques and instruments. The romance and nostalgia of the accordion, so prominent on the first record, was gone, replaced by a broad range of electric and acoustic keyboards and augmented by whatever a song called for: electric guitar, bass clarinet, trumpet, marimba, strings.

"Her approach to music is like nothing I'd ever seen," says Rick Haworth, a veteran of the Quebec club circuit who got a call to play guitar on the album and subsequently toured with Lhasa. "A lot more holding back than letting go. The silences were at least as important as the sounds. I had never worked on dynamics as much."

They might start with the most basic sounds and ideas, as when François beat on his chest to create the thumping rhythm of footfalls that drives "Anywhere on This Road." Next came wind chimes, temple bells, and atmospheric sound effects lifted from the soundtrack to a Mongolian film, capped off by a trumpet solo as mysterious and brittle as winter starlight played by the renowned Lebanese-French musician Ibrahim Maalouf. The resulting music sounded like nothing so much as a mashup of jazz trumpeter Don Cherry and Tibetan monks, while Lhasa, whose increased sophistication, confidence, and extraordinary ability to invest her lyrics with the kiss of life surprised even other vocalists. "She's just singing from the marrow of her bones," marveled Canadian singing star Feist.[3]

But the album's final track and the last one penned, "Soon This Space Will Be Too Small," suggested a desire to sing from an even more intimate, more molecular level. A breakthrough composition and a song like no other—a huge song about transcendence and acceptance, about life and death, and about belonging in the end to the universe— it achieves Lhasa's artistic grail: an apprehension and conveyance of the inexpressible. It also gave her the album title that had so far eluded her:

Soon this space will be too small
And I'll go outside
To the huge hillside
Where the wild winds blow
And the cold stars shine
I'll put my foot
On the living road
And be carried from here
To the heart of the world . . .

Not surprisingly, the song had its genesis in an ongoing philosophic discussion with her father, as she would relay in concert. "My father is a great philosopher," she liked to say by way of introducing the song. "He always has a big idea floating around and around in his mind for six or seven or eight years. And then, when he's really finished with that idea, he has a new idea. I'm going to tell you his new idea. He says that when we're conceived and we appear in our mother's womb, we're like a tiny light in the darkness of the ether. And in the beginning, there's only silence and darkness and time doesn't exist, and it feels like we're there for a thousand years. But we grow.

"And as we grow, slowly we begin to feel sensations and touch the walls. And little by little we begin to hear sounds and feel shocks that come from outside. And as we grow more and more, the distance between ourselves and that outside world grows smaller and smaller and the shocks from that outside world get stronger and stronger. And finally, this place we're in that felt so immense at the beginning has become very uncomfortable and then we have to be born. My father says that the moment of our birth is so chaotic and violent that all of us think, *this is it—I'm dying.* And then—what a surprise! It's only the beginning.

"And in the beginning, we're very small and the world feels infinitely large and our lives infinitely long. And we keep growing and using our senses and bodies and learn how to touch the walls and contours of this new world. And sometimes mixed in with all the sounds and sensations of this life, we hear sounds and feel shocks that come from outside. And that other world outside is just on the other side of a very thin wall. So thin, almost transparent and permeable, that it's possible for things to blast through and all our lives we're receiving things that pass through. And then, finally, this body becomes very uncomfortable and we have to die, too. And we think, again, *this is it—this is the end*. But my father says that's not the end, either. It's just the moment when we pass through that very thin wall and go live something else.

"A couple of months ago, I saw my father and he heard me tell this story and he said, 'It's very nice that you're telling that story. But you're forgetting the most important part. You have to say also that in the same way when we're in our mother's womb and developing organs and limbs that we have absolutely no use for where we are but will only be able to use afterwards, we're also developing an organ that's very awkward to use here in this life. And that's what our soul is.' In the same way, our energy is going to develop this thing that we don't really know what do with yet. But he believes that one day we will know what to do with it."

Wrapping stories and metaphors around songs would become a sizeable part of Lhasa's performance "She was a storyteller—that's how I always think of her," says her sister, Gabriela de la Vega. "That was her true purpose, not to be a singer or performer but to be a storyteller. She had to tell these stories." Nor was it coincidental that some of her most affecting stories came out of conversations with her father. "She learned a lot from her father and the way to express it captivatingly," says her friend and road manager, David-Etienne Savoie. "Her father has a way of telling stories and people love to listen. Lhasa learned from him."

The entire family was grist for her mill. "I once told Lhasa a story about a terrible love I'd had," says Ayin. "How I'd written it down on a piece of paper and gone to the ocean and thrown it in the water. And the next day there was a tsunami." When Ayin told the story, it was about the pain of the affair. But when she heard Lhasa recount the same story months later in concert, it had morphed into something humorous. "Everybody would laugh. And it was great because I was really feeling sorry for myself— as if the tsunami validated that this was the hardest relationship anyone had ever had."

Released at the end of 2003, *The Living Road* was greeted warmly in Canada and France, where Lhasa's nearly seven-year pause between albums proved inconsequential to fans and critics. Ostensibly released in the United States on the Nettwerk label, the album went unreviewed and unremarked. But in the United Kingdom, it was greeted with unreserved critical acclaim. As in France, where journalist Anne-Marie Paquotte had initially been instrumental in drumming up support for her and *La Llorona*, Lhasa and *The Living Road* now found an ardent and influential advocate in journalist and BBC world music programmer Charlie Gillett, whose enthusiasm led to the BBC naming her the 2005 Best Artist of the Americas in its World Music Awards.[4] The *Times* of London followed that by naming *The Living Road* one of the ten best world music albums of the decade, while the *Telegraph* declared her "world music's discovery of the year." Noting a "poetic intensity that combines a steely strength with a fascination for the mythical," *Telegraph* critic Peter Culshaw characterized Lhasa's songs as "deceptively simple—seemingly obvious, even—but when you unpack them they are quite radical and profound, things no one else seems to be saying."[5] Declared the *Guardian*, "Here, surely, is a multi-lingual global diva."[6]

The questions and doubts that led Lhasa to suspend her career were gone. "I love this life," she gushed to a reporter while touring Europe in support of *The Living Road*. "I love writing songs, I love recording them, I love singing them, and I love traveling. It's a wonderful life. I even love interviews! I think I was born to be a singer."

Before embarking on a three-month European tour, Lhasa made an important addition to her band. Montreal cellist Mélanie Auclair was a fan but had never met Lhasa. When the singer phoned out of the blue to ask if she was interested in playing on the tour, she quickly agreed but was taken aback nonetheless. "I didn't play on your album," she said. "You know that, right?"

"The cello player can't make the tour and I'm searching for a replacement," Lhasa replied. "Can we meet?"

There would be no audition. Instead, Mélanie met Lhasa and Gina Brault in a café (Gina, her marriage to Yves notwithstanding, remained Lhasa's manager). "We talked and talked and talked," says Mélanie. "I think Lhasa just wanted to know me, the human. She called me the next day and just said, 'Okay, let's do this.'"

Similarly, guitarist Rick Haworth had played on *The Living Road* but barely knew Lhasa and was surprised when she called and asked him to take over the guitar spot previously held by Yves. "This woman says so little—so when she called me I thought, *Really? I guess I didn't suck*," he says. "She also chose the keyboard player because we said he was good—never heard a note. What she would do instead was sit down with you and drink tea and decide, *These are people I want to be in a vehicle with*. Which is an extremely intelligent way of choosing your band. You spend a *lot* of time together."

Having Mélanie in the band was a needed change for Lhasa. She had felt isolated on previous tours—most nights, the guys in the band had partied while Lhasa slept and rested her voice. She wanted things to be different this time. It wasn't unusual for Mélanie and Lhasa to duck out together an hour before sound check.

"Speed shopping," says Mélanie. "She was the kind of girl to buy me a new pair of shoes because I was sad that day. Or show up with miso soup. She was like a very good big sister. She took care of me."

Though an easy traveler—her childhood had conditioned her to spend long journeys with her head in a book—Lhasa put all she had into each performance.

"Her intentions were very unusual—with her, it's very, very special," says David-Etienne Savoie. "I've been touring for twenty years with amazing artists and I've never experienced one who was similar. She had a lot of empathy and believed in the healing force of music. Sometimes artists are a little selfish—and I'm not saying she wasn't. But the way she wanted to connect, and what she wanted to do with her music, was to open people's minds to mysteries, magic, and the resonance between us and the universe. Focusing us on the spiritual part of life. Not religious, but an opening to what this experience of life is. She wanted to touch every person's heart and blow their mind, even if it was a show that could be considered less important. She would go to that zone every night. And every night I enjoyed seeing her perform." It was the same experience for the musicians.

"It wasn't just her voice but her whole body," says Mélanie. "Watching her was so intense."

"The most amazing thing for me was the way she sang and interpreted every note," says Erik. "She felt every note—it was mind-blowing, the kind of focus she had onstage. She wrote very nice songs, but her real power was as a singer onstage and the way she could move everybody with very slow songs. Really slow tempos, and sometimes hard to play."

That empathy and intensity, and her appreciation and veneration of music from the heart, enabled Lhasa to move across boundaries of genre and culture. It didn't matter where the music was from—she performed songs from Russia, Mexico, Syria, Spain, Turkey, the United States, Italy, Lebanon, France, England, Chechnya, and

Venezuela—she recognized and kept what was real, discarding what was not.

Lhasa was particularly excited when she got the chance to play her first date in Portugal, the homeland of fado, the emotionally charged tragic songs of love and loss she adored. To mark the occasion, she and the band prepared a version of a classic fado ballad, "Meu Limao de Amargura (Meu Amor, Meu Amor)" ("My Bitter Lemon [My Love, My Love]"), associated with one of the tradition's great divas, Amália Rodrigues. But the afternoon they arrived in Lisbon, the promoter cornered David-Etienne Savoie. He cautioned that it might not go over the way Lhasa envisioned.

"Are you sure she wants to do that fado song?" he asked. "Normally people think it pleases us to come and do fado, but they don't get that it's a sacred music for us. The reaction can be rude—they might not like it. Just so you know, it's tricky."

While assuring the promoter that there was nothing to worry about, David wasn't actually so sure. *It's not my culture*, he thought. *Maybe they won't like it.*

He needn't have worried.

"When she sang it, you could hear a fly in the room," David says. "And when she finished, there was a huge standing ovation. I still have shivers thinking about that moment. Lhasa only played seven shows in Portugal. Yet, when she passed away, several of the national newspapers put it on the front page."

Lhasa took to including the ballad in her repertoire. A tormented song that likens love to grief and suffering— a "millstone of tenderness," a "ship of torture"—its final wrenching stanza translates, "We don't know how to swim / And we die, we die / Slowly, slowly." She reached for it at a music festival in Switzerland when asked to dedicate a song to a festival volunteer killed in a motorcycle accident. "He went home the night before and died on the road," says David. "So she sang the Amália Rodrigues song for him. And at the moment when she sang 'And we die' all the power shut off."

With just eight bars left to perform in the song, the band didn't know what to do. "We can hear the music from the other stages," says Rick. "Just our tent is gone. The crew is running around madly trying to find the breakers and get the generators going. We left the stage for twenty-five minutes but the audience—three thousand people—are just standing there and will not move. When the electricity came back on and we came out, she didn't go into the next song—we ended that one. The audience went ballistic and I'm thinking, *She's connected, man*. It was insane. I'm older than Lhasa and really conservative. Yet, I would literally weep when Mélanie and I played the trio version of 'Soon This Space Will Be Too Small' with her. I don't believe in magic; I'm extremely rational. But the things I witnessed with this woman? If somebody told me she came from another planet, I might be able to buy it."

Recharging required time and solitude. "The bar was very high and we couldn't book more than four shows a week," David says. If the band had a few days off, they might retreat to an old hotel in Marseille overlooking the Mediterranean that Lhasa liked to use as their home base. And on the road, she asked David to try to avoid chain hotels. "The vibe of a place was important to her and she liked old places—places that were beautiful, had history, were inspiring." The band usually congregated in the soundman's room—generally a larger suite with a balcony for just that reason. And while Lhasa might pop in for a beer, she spent most of her time alone in her room.

"She read a lot, lot, *lot*," says David. "More than anyone I've been on the road with. She would sit next to me in a van and read for hours, page after page after page." She also had a few guilty pleasures for unwinding. A serious cinephile, she particularly loved the films of Andrei Tarkovsky and Satyajit Ray and even painted a portrait of Ray to hang in her home. On the road, though, she reached for decidedly lighter fare, feeding an addiction to the television series *24* and indulging her giggly side with teen comedies. Her favorite was *Legally Blonde*, and she would watch it at the drop of a hat. "She was so silly," says her friend, Sandra Khouri. "*So* silly."

But no matter how much Lhasa tried to rest and nurture her voice offstage, her dramatic style of singing was taking a toll. Incorporating the emotional delivery and rustic tics of Mexican music, she had set herself apart in Montreal and on *La Llorona* by singing with a brokenhearted cry, which pushed her voice and strained her vocal chords. Even more damaging was a penchant for favoring arrangements in a lower range—she liked the powerful, dramatic effect it had, especially on slow songs—and she often reached for notes that weren't really in her range. The problem became more serious when her voice gave out completely after a show in Paris.

A leading Parisian throat specialist diagnosed nodes on her vocal chords and prescribed surgery; Lhasa didn't want to hear it. Instead, David-Etienne Savoie took her to a voice coach in the French countryside. The daughter of an opera singer, the instructor was well versed in classical techniques but also dispensed common sense, convincing Lhasa that she had been singing too low and needed to immediately raise the key on several songs. And going forward, she had to find a more natural, less strenuous style of singing. "She completely changed Lhasa's perspective," he says. "After that, what she wanted to do changed. She decided she didn't want to continue with that dramatic style and was looking for other musicians to help her."

On break between tours, Lhasa surprised everyone by purchasing a home in Montreal—a large stone row house on Rue de l'Esplanade in Mile End. "Lhasa with roots?" says Rick. "*That's* something new. Yet, that was a place she felt so comfortable." More than that, she became a face around the neighborhood, swimming and hitting the steam room at the YMCA nearly every day. She was easy to spot in cafes or on the street in the old-fashioned black leather aviator helmet she wore through Montreal's long winters.

"Her place was very inspiring. A lot of photographs of her family and ancestors. Plants, cats, books, paintings, objects. It smelled good," says David-Etienne Savoie. "There was a true atmosphere of silence at her place," says Arthur H. "And when you entered, you felt a kind of calm—maybe because of the photographs of her Lebanese great-grandfather and her grandmother, who was an actress. All very beautiful big black-and-white pictures."[7]

Patrick Watson also felt it. "Time stopped when you were at Lhasa's house," he says. "It was a bit like Narnia, walking into the wardrobe. Her house had a very patient and detailed feeling to it. It was like going into a different time. She had a TV that she kept under a blanket and that made me laugh. 'You watch TV?' 'Nope.'"

Lhasa's friend and collaborator Sarah Pagé recalls an evening at the house when Lhasa was deep in conversation and unaware that a spider was crawling closer and closer to her head. "I'm getting worried and about to say, "'Uh, Lhasa . . . ,'" when she happened to look. 'Oh, a little friend!' And immediately went off on a track about what this spider was coming to tell her. It was her interpretation of the world around her. If you were encountering her and she was encountering you, for her it was a given that you were meant to be there at that moment. So you're immediately confronted with someone who is not attributing magical powers to themselves, but to *you*. And because she was so generous in that way, it made people want to reciprocate. You'd feel you'd give her anything."

Yet, Lhasa could also be combative and contrarian and frequently fell out with friends. Whether discussing music, books, film, or painting, she had strong opinions regarding what was good and bad and wasn't shy about sharing or defending them—as her friend Lousnak Abdalian, who also painted, could attest.

"We used to have very peppery discussions about art," she says. "We were like cats and dogs; we fought a lot." Indeed, Lhasa didn't hesitate to tell Lousnak that her paintings lacked perspective—in either concept or execution. "She went all the way! It drove me crazy. And one day when we were having this conversation, I just walked away. But that was us. Two days later, we're right back—it's love again, no problem. A lot of people misunderstood because in Montreal people don't like to argue much. But if you don't argue then you don't hear what you're thinking and critique yourself. We used to argue about art a lot. *A lot*." Between fights, Lhasa also painted a portrait of Lousnak as a gift. "It was the first time I'd had my portrait done and I cried when I saw it. It's not me necessarily, but it's me totally. You understand?"

If it was hard to hear her criticism, it was also clear that Lhasa wanted to know the unvarnished truth about her own work. When she finished a new painting, she was eager to know what Lousnak thought—but had a unique and unsparing method for finding out. Lhasa would keep the new painting covered until Lousnak was in front of it and wouldn't unveil it until she was in a position to watch her friend's reaction. "She used to read my face the first time I saw a painting to try and know what I'm really thinking. She wasn't satisfied with her painting. At the end, she started doing abstracts based on music."

And she could be just as critical with friends in the music world.

"She was very meticulous," says Patrick: "A super perfectionist. We had a friendship that was not cold but realistic. She'd be hard and I'd be hard. She'd say, 'You gotta work on your fucking lyrics.' And I'd say, 'Why do you give the same goddamn speech every night before a song? It bores me to death.' We were hard on each other; we had a real thing. People paint her in a la-la way and don't know how ambitious she was and how much of a businesswoman she was."

She published a short book of reflections in French, *La route chante* (*The Road Sings*), in 2008 and expected to write more. She was forced to put aside a fantasy adventure novel when she became ill.

Her myriad interests and abilities could leave Lhasa feeling conflicted, saying she needed to focus her attention exclusively on music. Her friend Ralph Dfouni disagreed. "She told me many times, 'I am a singer, I want to accept that, nothing more,'" he says. "I gave her an Indian desk on one of her birthdays. It was small, like a school desk that opens up. I told her I was giving it to her because I thought she was a poet and writer more than anything else, more than a musician."

The house also became home at times for her brother, Mischa, and sister, Eden, both in their early twenties and twelve years younger than Lhasa. Mischa had been going through a difficult time, bouncing between his father, the San Francisco political activist and antiquarian bookseller Mike Pincus, and Alexandra in Marseille, when he reconnected with Lhasa. "I was kind of lost and had nothing going on," he says. "And in one of her signature strokes of generosity and insight, she invited me on tour with her. I was playing guitar at the time and she said, 'Come with me and play a couple of songs with the band.' I wasn't on the tour long, but we started to know each other and get along." When Lhasa bought the house, she invited Mischa to come live there, which he did before getting his own place in the neighborhood. "I got a job, started working and living my life, and she was part of it, definitely more than any other sister I have. We'd meet for coffee and talk about her struggles and her existential crises." He adds with a laugh, "Of which there were many."

Like Mischa, Eden found a needed welcome at a low moment. "I was living in Montreal and pretty off my rocker," she says. "My parents were like, *we don't even know what to do with you*. I looked up to Lhasa. When I was born she was living with my parents and always had a very motherly relationship with me—and she was the perfect mother for me at the time: totally cool about the many weird things I was doing. I had no money and she was insanely generous. She gave me gifts and took care of me and knew I needed someone to talk to and eat with. We spent a lot of time just sitting around her table, smoking Benson & Hedges and talking. And drinking tea. She was very into drinking tea. And she would do that and not make any judgments about what I was or was not doing with my life. When I was in trouble she took care of me."

Yet, Lhasa's personal life remained a puzzle she couldn't quite piece together. She was a hardcore romantic, but her successful career, powerful personality, and deep focus made it difficult to picture her with a partner. "It would have been really tough to find a good match for Lhasa," says Patrick. "When you walk into her house, you can't really imagine her living harmoniously. The place had such a strong presence—you would have to be a bit invisible to fit in. A real partner would have been almost impossible to find."

Through Bïa and Erik, who had also come back to Montreal, Lhasa met Thomas Hellman. Then an up-and-coming singer-songwriter working in both English and French, he subsequently became a successful recording artist and on-air columnist for *Radio-Canada*, the French arm of the Canadian Broadcasting Company. Their year-long relationship was no day at the beach. It was more like life on the open sea: some days beautiful and calm, others tumultuous and raging.

"She wasn't the easiest person to deal with," Hellman says. "But to sing like that you have to have a beautiful soul. When you have a soul that huge, life is going to be difficult. You're going to have difficult relationships with people."

The first few months were idyllic: they played piano, listened to Al Green and Bob Dylan, drank tea—Lhasa drank endless cups of chai tea with soy milk throughout the day—and read passages from Jung to each other. "We had long conversations," he says. "Very long conversations." They went out in the evenings to visit friends, hear music, and see movies. They took trips together, driving to Boston or to his family's cabin in Quebec's Laurentian Mountains, where she sang him a new song she had written, "I'm Going In." "It was really moving," says Hellman. "Just the two of us, pretty early in the relationship, sitting by the fire drinking beers."

Five years her junior, he was surprised to find she'd had very little experience with men. "From what I understood, they were strange relationships: it was always very intense, very dramatic, and with very little intimacy. But she really wanted to be with someone. Intimacy actually was amazing for her, but letting go was difficult. There was a part of her that didn't like depending on anyone; she was very much about having control and independence. In the end, a lot of our relationship worked—and I think it was the first time she had a relationship that worked."

Following her lead, Hellman learned how to cull images from dreams in his work. "It's a real source and I owe her for that," he says. "She felt that dreams were guiding her and the imagery was part of her work. You can hear it on *The Living Road* and also on the last album. The song 'A Fish on Land' is a dream from beginning to end."

He was less enthusiastic about some of her other views—so much so that it led to fights. "She believed that she was being guided, that the universe cares. There were people in her life pushing her in that direction. I tried to get her to read existentialists because I believe in the absurd and that the universe doesn't give a damn about any of us. And I'd say to her, 'I'm sorry, but I can't accept that the universe is this way and that you're guided in this direction. I just don't believe in it.' And that would piss her off so much that she would throw me out of the house and not speak to me for a while."

He also found her reliance on the *I Ching* disquieting, in part because it was often linked with bouts of doubt and stormy moods. Though Lhasa faulted her mother for creating dramatic, tempestuous scenes that affected the family and upset life, she seemed unable to completely break the pattern.

"She would push people away—it was almost as if her relationships had to be based on some form of drama," Hellman says. "She'd get dark. And when she got dark, she was a mix of proud and insecure. She would ask herself questions about whatever relationship she was having or what move to make in her career, and she would do the *I Ching* obsessively. It got pretty far out."

Even Eden, who worshiped her sister and completely understood and related to her spirituality, could be left bewildered. "She subscribed to a magazine called *The Fortean Times*," she says. "It's so out there—it's borderline insane. It had articles like '*Did* Aliens Build the Pyramids?' 'Lhasa, really?' 'I dunno.'"[8]

Sturm und Drang may have been genetically encoded in the Karam DNA, but it wasn't for Hellman. The unbridgeable issue, however, was that they were at different points in their lives. The real doubts began when Lhasa declared herself ready to start a family. Fresh out of graduate school, Thomas was just beginning his career and couldn't see himself settling down. He also found Lhasa's sudden urgency disquieting: her work was of paramount importance to her and she could ruminate ceaselessly, even after she had set a course. Would she say something completely different in a month?

"She was really torn over how tied to reality she wanted to be," says Eden: "Whether to live a more monastic, spiritual existence, where the most important thing is where your head is at, or to have a relationship and a house and a child and those things. It's hard to live in both of those worlds at the same time, especially for a woman. She wanted to find someone and be sure of them, wanted to have children with them. But she would go back and forth. She got this big house and fixed it up and really liked it. But she would say, 'Yeah, . . . I keep picturing myself in a small apartment way up high with all windows and lots of light and getting rid of my house.' It's hard to generate material when you're focused on something like having a relationship or children or a house. Or a more normal life. And I don't think she knew how to navigate those two paths." In the end it was moot: Thomas wasn't ready for children.

"It was mostly great," he says of their time together. "She could be very intense, but she was also amazing. I think of her as one of the great encounters of my life. And that comes with a price."

It came with a price for Lhasa as well.

"I think she was deeply, deeply disappointed in love and it was so very vital to her," says Sarah Pagé. "She had turned herself into this great singer and, in her mind, into the princess. And still no prince appeared. And, in fact, some of the men in her life held her status and grandness against her. They would punish her in little ways here and there."

Life seemed surer on the road, where the resonance Lhasa sought was evident each night in concert, and her touring band fiercely loyal. "We didn't know Thomas Hellman," says Rick, "but we didn't like him. He made Lhasa cry."

In Europe, she had a widening circle of friends and collaborators who understood her. Along with Arthur H, she had developed a close friendship with Bratsch, the French Gypsy band that she and Yves admired. They backed her on a French television appearance, and she sang a Russian lullaby, "Nié Boutidié" ("Don't Wake the Sun") on one of their albums. And the English singer and composer Stuart A. Staples reached out to her when his group, Tindersticks, was looking for a female vocalist for the duet "Sometimes it Hurts." Though he didn't know her, Staples had been blown away by *La Llorona* and called her cold. They discovered they had a lot in common. Like Lhasa, his interests and work were wide-ranging and individual. Aside from playing with Tindersticks, he created a musical soundscape for the In Flanders Fields Museum, the permanent exhibition of the World War I memorial in Ypres, Belgium. He is an accomplished composer and producer of film soundtracks, including six for celebrated French filmmaker Claire Denis. Prior to working with Lhasa, Staples wrote and recorded a duet with Isabella Rossellini. A Francophile, Staples had resettled in La Souterraine in the rural Limousin region, and he and his wife, the English-born painter Suzanne Osborne, grew close to Lhasa. She would record two more duets with him, "That Leaving Feeling" and "Hey, Lucinda." "The moment we met her we kind of clicked," says Staples. "There was an understanding—a deeper musical understanding—that we had. It really gave me a lot over the years."[9]

In concert, Lhasa's band continued to marvel at the synchronicity churning in her wake. At the Istanbul International Jazz Festival, a huge citywide event, they found themselves playing an outdoor venue alongside a bridge connecting Asia and Europe. "While we were playing, they were putting train cars on a ferry between the two continents and you could hear this screeching, grinding metal in the distance," says Rick Haworth. "And it worked perfectly with 'Anywhere on This Road.' Trust me, all this weird stuff never happens in a show. In Spain, church bells rang at the right moment."

One night after a show, Lhasa asked Mélanie to come into her hotel room.

"Could you do me a favor?" Lhasa asked. "It feels like I've got a lump in my breast. Would you take a look and tell me what you think?" Mélanie thought there was something there.

Back home, Lhasa saw a doctor who diagnosed it as a benign cyst. Relieved, she continued to work.

Creating a smaller, intimate trio show with Mélanie and Rick, Lhasa played a string of dates in the United States in 2005. Still virtually unknown in her native country, she was performing in smaller venues like Chicago's Hot-House and art spaces, including the Andy Warhol Museum in Pittsburgh and Boston's Museum of Fine Arts. Though local reviews and newspaper profiles in the United States were unfailingly effusive, she didn't have the same luck with the national rock press, which largely failed to notice her. One of the few reviews in an American music magazine came via *Spin*, where Will Hermes characterized her as a "drama queen" employing "Spanish sibilants that splay like Tori Amos's knees."[10] Recommending the trio at Symphony Space, *New Yorker* pop critic Sasha Frere-Jones had a perceptive, poetic read on Lhasa: "Her contralto voice is what folks call husky," he wrote, "but what it sounds like is a large orange sun, burnt at the edges and going down." Still, he seemed to find some of her performance a little overcooked. He was captivated by Mélanie's playing, crediting her with leavening things by "wordlessly adding humor to de Sela's dark invocations" and nearly stealing the show.[11]

As always, Lhasa took her time between albums. "There was a whole wave she had to go through each time," says Mischa. "Album, recording release, lots and lots of touring, success, fatigue, moving somewhere or, later, coming back home. And then she'd question everything she had done and really wipe herself completely clean in order to make a new album based on her subsequent ideas and learning. It was a long process of regeneration."

Four years after the release of *The Living Road*, she made arrangements to return to France to record some of the new songs she had written. On the eve of that trip, she was to fly to New York to sing as a guest with the group Calexico, having befriended and collaborated with their singer, Joey Burns. Getting into the cab for the airport, she suddenly asked the driver to wait a moment, and she bounded back up the snow-encrusted stairs and into the house. She had forgotten to say good-bye to Isaan, her cat. In the vestibule, she slipped and fell, shattering bones in her ankle. The injury required more than just a cast. A rod and steel screws had to be inserted to help the bones knit and she spent a week in the hospital; Mélanie prepared food for her and kept her company.

Though the break was unusually severe, she didn't give in to convalescence. "Bïa loved it when both of them were singing together," says Erik. "And we were playing one night in a tiny place with a high stage. Lhasa comes from the back of the hall on one foot and she climbs up like three feet—just jumps on one leg: *Bam! Okay, I'm ready to sing.* She was a very surprising person," he says with a laugh.

At dinner at Patrick Watson's loft one evening, Lhasa met Sarah Pagé, a harpist who had attended music school with Watson and was branching beyond classical into contemporary music, most often with her neighbors, the guitarist Brad Barr and his brother Andrew, a drummer. Sarah was in the midst of shaking off a busted romance, while Lhasa, with her faith that there are no accidents in the universe, was ruminating on what it meant that her fall hadn't allowed her to start work on her album in France. Each considered herself at a crossroads, and the two women took to calling each other to commiserate. They were soon meeting daily at Lhasa's house, writing and playing music together.

In the wake of her fall, Lhasa's thoughts and "regeneration" began to come into focus. She needed to simplify her singing style—it was clear that she couldn't continue taxing her voice the way she had on the earlier records and tours—but she also wanted to simplify the overall sound of her music, as well as her role onstage and as a bandleader. "Being a singer that so many people just adored and projected so much onto became exhausting," says Sarah. "She was tired of carrying all the weight; she wanted to feel like she was in a band."

It also irked her to be placed on the world music stage at festivals. As she had noted in interviews, her music was chiefly an outgrowth of what she had heard during her childhood; as far as she was concerned, what she wrote and performed was "just music." "It produced some frustration from time to time," says Rick. "She did not consider herself a world music artist. She considered herself an artist."

And last, but certainly not least, was her desire to find an audience in her homeland.

"She was frustrated," says Patrick. "She wanted to be heard in the States. We had a lot of business discussions because we were both bandleaders and she was very ambitious. Lhasa was 100 percent integrity, but you can't be successful like that without being a businesswoman. She could make the hard decisions. She knew what she was doing every time."

Singing in Spanish and French, she could reach audiences in Europe and Canada, but not in the United States. All the songs for the next album were written in English, and as far as finding the musicians to craft a sound, Mile End had what she needed. The musicians in this young, Anglo neighborhood were very much in tune with the American alt-rock scene; several local bands, most notably Wolf Parade and Arcade Fire, were on the cusp of US stardom. Lhasa asked Sarah to recommend musicians she knew from playing around town, and she introduced Lhasa to an outstanding bassist, Miles Perkins. The three were soon meeting for coffee daily and hitting the bars every night, and they began rehearsing with drummer Andrew Barr and guitarist Joe Grass, who also played pedal steel guitar. The new lineup had a much more straightforward sound. It essentially gave Lhasa a standard vocalist's backing quartet with a unique twist: instead of piano, there was a harp—the instrument Alexandra played and the first one Lhasa had sung along with as a child. And, as in country music, the pedal steel could suggest strings.

Though rehearsals were originally slow as the band sought to articulate the musical feeling she wanted to convey in each song, they soon found their footing. "We called the way she wrote *poom-plinks*," Grass says. "Playing the piano with one finger on the left hand, one finger on the right. But she had an amazing sense of melody and knew the feeling she wanted and guided the music quite clearly.

We would take those simple things and run with them, find the right colors." She also urged Joe not to overplay. "I learned a lot playing with her: help the color, help the arrangement."

Mélanie knew Lhasa had been checking out the Mile End scene. "She wanted to be part of that," she says. But when Lhasa called and asked her to drop by the house, she still wasn't prepared for the inevitable. Over dinner in a nearby restaurant, Lhasa gave her the news.

"I have to tell you," she said, "I'm working with other musicians. And maybe I'll work with another cello player."[12]

"'*Non!* No, no, no—*please!*' It was really so hard," Mélanie recalls. "Heartbreaking. I respect her—I respect the vision—but for me personally, it was really difficult. And what's hardest is that I know I am going to lose my privileged place in her heart. We had a relationship after that; we were friends. But it's not the same."

In moving on artistically, Lhasa was once again presented with the unavoidable reality of disappointing and hurting friends. But as she discovered with Yves, she had the strength and temperament to look in and follow the work, even at the price of sentiment.

"Part of the problem was that she needed other people to do what she did and it was difficult for those others to find the healthy limit of their relationship with Lhasa," says Patrick. "So it causes a lot of pain. You would get involved with her from the heart and soul—everybody who met her instantly felt like she was their best friend because of the type of person she was. But she could say, 'This is still my music' and break a lot of hearts. A lot of hearts. The boundary was a really tricky thing for Lhasa because everyone wanted to be inside her bubble all the time. Including her family, including her friends. And that was a huge dilemma and hard for her. I'm 100 percent sure Sarah's relationship with Lhasa would have ended very poorly. I've seen her flush people; she flushed me. It didn't affect us in the same way because I've got a band and I know what it means."

Lhasa also informed drummer François Lalonde, who coproduced her first two albums, that she intended to produce this album herself. However, she added that she had an idea for another album she would like to do in the future—to be recorded in South America with musicians from several countries—and that she hoped he would come with her and produce that.

To help develop a more natural and less forced singing style, Lhasa took lessons with Johanne Raby, the voice coach for the Montreal pop singer Celine Dion. Raby taught her to sing in a way that opened her voice. And with her eye on developing her career beyond Canada and Europe, Lhasa also opted to end her management agreement with Gina, who could offer little in the way of experience or contacts in the American music business.

More than ever, Lhasa was taking control of her career and life. After dating the actor Gael García Bernal, she had begun a serious relationship with Ryan Morey, a remix engineer who had grown up in Montreal and lived around the corner. A fan, he would shyly say hello if he saw her on the street or in the coffee shop. Seeing her looking blue one day, he asked what was wrong. She had lost tracks she was working on in a computer fire. They talked shop and commiserated. Sometime later they ran into each other at a box-wine party following a dance performance and spoke some more; he screwed up his courage and asked a friend for her number. Though she agreed to meet at a small club, he went with a mix of excitement and intimidation. "I wasn't really sure," Ryan says. "I was still on the larger-than-life side." He got to the club early, just as a dramatic downpour began. A few minutes later, Lhasa rode up to the club on a bicycle, soaked to the bone. "She was a really good sport about it and that brought her down to earth in my eyes. We were together from that point."

Friends and family noted a new confidence.

"I always used to be a little annoyed at her," says her older sister, Gabriela. *C'mon, man! You have some money— wear some beautiful shoes. Shoes are so much fun!* Both sisters were enjoying success: Gabriela's jewelry design business in New York had taken off—she had her own counter in Barney's—and Lhasa would come down from Montreal for shopping trips. "We would find stuff for her shows," Gabriela says. "Her identity onstage evolved, and I would encourage her to have fun. It was wonderful to collaborate with her because she had money to spend on that stuff and she was sophisticated. And once she got into it, she *really* got into it! She ended up loving sparkly things and sequins—not tacky things. She developed her own tastes. It was fun to be part of that: the freedom of it and realizing its part of how you say who you are onstage. It is a visual medium as well." Her friend Bïa also saw the change: her "little wet bird" had flown.

"She was eating up life," Bïa says. "She was in love and happy with Ryan. Before, she would get angry if someone said, 'You're a very beautiful girl.' *Hey, it's not about the looks.* But she got comfortable in her body and womanhood. She was really loved—she met someone who liked her. Because people would admire her or maybe want a piece of her or not understand and take her the wrong way. With Ryan, she was with someone who thought she was witty and funny and intelligent and special. As a person. And that was nourishing: she was in a very good place as a woman and physically transformed. She was so beautiful—her hair, her skin, her back was straight, and her walk was determined. She started dressing and becoming a coquette. She came to my house and said, 'Hey, look at me—I have a red coat!' And we laughed because it was an adventure for her to have something that wasn't black. She was beaming and for the first time in her life felt she was in the right place and doing her own thing. *Okay! I'm a woman now! No one is telling me what to do or putting me in that uniform that doesn't fit. It's me here, guys! I'm having a laugh, writing songs about my ex-boyfriends, my life, and my dreams and visions.* At that moment, she was at the apex of her life."

— 5 —

BELLS

I had a dream last night
A fish on land
Gasping for breath
Just laughed
And sang this song
Is life like this for everyone?
Is life like this for everyone?

LHASA DE SELA,
"A Fish on Land"

Writing in cafes had long been a feature of Lhasa's routine, and Club Social on Rue St-Viateur became her usual roost. Bassist Thierry Amar also lived in the neighborhood, and he would run into her there. As a member of several bands—including Godspeed You! Black Emperor and Thee Silver Mt. Zion Memorial Orchestra—Amar had helped build a vibrant, sophisticated, free-standing, and independent music community. It included a label, Constellation Records, and a studio, Hotel2Tango, located about two blocks from Club Social. Lhasa told Amar she hoped to record and produce her next album there live to tape and asked if he would help. He agreed, ultimately playing some upright bass, mixing the album, and co-engineering it with Howard Bilerman. "She was feeling a bit claustrophobic and decided to take matters in her own hands," Amar says of Lhasa's decision to produce herself. "She was ready to do a record without a producer in the language of her choice."

Rehearsing the band and preparing to record, Lhasa received an unexpected call in early 2008 from Roscoe Beck, the bassist and musical director for Leonard Cohen. The legendary Montreal singer-songwriter needed a backup singer for his upcoming world tour. Would she be interested in coming to the rehearsals starting in Los Angeles in two weeks to audition? Cohen, of course, had long been one of her idols: in her early days in Montreal, Lhasa would leave snow angels in front of his house; in concert, she had covered "Who by Fire." Working with Cohen would be a chance for Lhasa, as a songwriter and performer, to attend a very special, exclusive school—and for that, she would be willing to postpone recording her next album. She agreed to come and audition.

She hadn't been feeling right, however. Following an examination and tests, she received a shock: she had breast cancer. Following the diagnosis, the old film from her biopsy and exam two years prior was re-examined. It revealed that while the first tumor was indeed benign, observable conditions in the surrounding tissue should have been a tip-off that she was particularly susceptible to cancer and needed to be monitored and vigilant. Now the cancer was well advanced, nearly Stage 4.

Ryan encouraged her to keep the audition date and explain the situation to Cohen. "She went and rehearsed for a few days and told him," he says. "No surprise, he was every bit the compassionate gentleman you would expect and told her to do whatever she needed to do. She came back unsure what that was."

Ultimately, she concluded that she had to put whatever energy she would have into her own work and apologetically declined Cohen's offer. If tinged with regret, it was the easiest decision she faced. Although uncertain what to do, Lhasa appeared both unfazed and not particularly interested in traditional medical treatment as word of her condition spread among family and friends.

"I was with her in the kitchen when she got her diagnosis," says Eden. "She said, 'Oh, I don't think this is going to be serious.' She never believed she would die." And when Lhasa told Eden she didn't want to have a mastectomy or undergo chemotherapy, her sister could only agree. "I worshiped the ground she walked on and didn't know shit about life or cancer or anything. I just knew she was my older sister and the coolest and smartest person in the world. And whatever she said was definitely right. *You want to get vitamin injections instead? Definitely! Totally do that!*"

Behind the casual confidence she displayed to Eden and others lay a secret Lhasa didn't want to share: she was terrified and furious. Told of the diagnosis, Alexandra immediately flew in from France. Lhasa gave her both barrels.

"She was in a rage and most of that came out at me," she says. "It was very primal, way beyond and before words. It was, *How could you do this to me? How could you bring me here for this?* It was very painful, but in a way it seemed so natural and didn't surprise me. The message was, *Well, you put me here—now save me.*" Perhaps most painful, Lhasa told her mother she didn't want her there. "So I went back to Marseille."

Bïa and Erik urged her to seek medical treatment immediately. Lhasa said she wanted to treat her condition naturally, and Bïa, with a brother in Brazil who is a doctor, fervently argued with her. "I called my friends who are doctors and nurses and asked, 'Who's the best in town?' I got her a meeting right away with a promise that she would have a private room for her chemo. And she was like, 'Whoa, whoa, whoa. I have to do some thinking.' I said, 'Forget about nature! Nature doesn't cure cancer—cancer is what nature found to get rid of us! Try the chemistry—that's what's making people too old for the planet, but that's what you need. Please, no carrot juice!' She was always very sweet with me, but it was, 'Yeah, but I need time.'" "For a good six to eight months she tried to work it out only with natural treatments," says Erik. "And that did not help."

Lhasa's intransigence left some perplexed and angry. "I was mad at her," says Patrick. "This Vitamin C bullshit. I can respect romance and the bubble. But there's a time to call a spade a spade. Smarten up and go get chemo."

Even within the family, opinions ran wide. Alejandro approved of Lhasa's decision to focus on faith healing and holistic treatments. Marybeth wasn't so sure and wanted Lhasa to see oncologists as well. Still, when Lhasa asked Marybeth to take her to see John of God, a Brazilian faith healer credited with miraculous healings who was visiting the United States, she agreed.

Her own skepticism notwithstanding, she, like Lhasa, found the morning service John conducted moving. "It was very much like what mass was like years ago in Mexico," Marybeth says. "Back then it was a very beautiful, very spiritual experience that had informed her and me and we both really liked it. The afternoon felt a bit hokier." It began with the healer meeting the hundreds of supplicants—everyone had to be dressed in white—many of whom were cancer sufferers. "You go in front of him and he decides who he will 'operate on' and who he will not 'operate on.' And then you got on another long line and he just touched you—'I'm operating on you.' And it's certainly an interesting experience for a skeptic like me: it gives you hope and makes you psychologically feel better and there's something to be said for that. It certainly didn't heal her."

Sarah, who saw that Lhasa did not respond to prods from Bïa and others—and, indeed, that Lhasa became loath to speak with anyone who disagreed with what she was doing—tried to walk a tightrope. Worried about the path Lhasa had chosen, she nonetheless hoped she might do more by holding her tongue. "She had a lot of friends who said something and she just stopped talking to them," Sarah says. "I think it actually would have been worse if she didn't have a couple of people around that she just could unload on. I would go over after her appointments or go with her. And she was always allowed to break down in front of me and cry because I was not going to tell her what to do. And I think Ryan filled that role as well; if she didn't have that, she would have been alone. She certainly wasn't going to listen to anyone." Even her brother, Mischa, could find her frustrating. "She had an ego and she had a capacity for thinking she knew things others didn't," he says.

Still, there came a day when an increasingly concerned Sarah, along with singer and friend Marie-Jo Thério, tried to prod Lhasa into beginning medical treatment by offering to accompany her to the hospital for a consultation. Lhasa had been stalling, saying she couldn't do anything until her files and film were transferred from the clinic to the hospital. After putting them off through the morning, Lhasa agreed but insisted they go to lunch first—and then sat in the café over the empty dishes for the better part of the afternoon. Six hours after broaching the subject, Sarah made a final push, noting that the clinic would still be open for another fifteen minutes and that they could get it done. But Lhasa proved obdurate. "She just broke down in tears in the restaurant," says Sarah. "And she said, 'I don't want to go.'"

Ryan strove to see it through her eyes.

"I don't know if I would qualify it as denial," he says. "That wasn't the quality of it. She didn't quite spurn treatment—she reasonably approached Cancer Inc. the way she did everything, not taking it on gospel. And she definitely sought alternative treatments. I think it was closer to being a personal and private struggle for her. That particular disease is always going to challenge somebody's core beliefs and it did so with Lhasa. It puts everything to the test, doesn't it?"

Clearly, one of the things it was testing was her belief in the primacy of the spirit: that had always been her core. "We talked a lot about faith," says Ayin. "At one point we were having a crisis. I was feeling betrayed and she was feeling betrayed. She said, 'Well, if trust is what we're trying to learn, why would we be given something that doesn't require it?'"

Even the few friends allowed to witness Lhasa's struggles couldn't agree on why she spurned medical treatment. Like Ayin, Sarah saw it as a desire not to betray her spiritual idealism, "her stubborn unwillingness to surrender to the body and the trap of being alive." But to Ralph Dfouni, who viewed Lhasa with a more pragmatic but no less loving eye, his friend simply found the notion of her own death overwhelming. "This one was too big," he said. "She didn't take care of anything."

Perhaps as daunting, Lhasa feared that committing to a medical program would lead inexorably to treatments that could cost her any chance of having children—something she now urgently desired.

In the midst of the crisis and attendant debate over what she should do, Lhasa still had an album to record. In her work she could pursue clarity and find answers: it was the oasis where the world still made sense and tomorrow remained hers to dictate. And for this album, her goal was direct simplicity—in melody, lyrics, and performance, particularly her vocals.

"She kept saying *The Living Road* was over-produced," says Ralph, "that she forced her voice to be beautiful. And to her, eliminating artifice meant being truer to herself. 'I'm just going to sing with my voice. Not with my image, just my voice.' And it's a big deal for a singer to stop doing something for which they are recognized. *Can I become natural rather than forced and still be me?* It was an important shift in her life."

Working live to tape was a way to stay focused on that task. With Jean and François on *The Living Road*, they had recorded digitally and employed popular studio programs such as Pro Tools, which make it easy to edit and manipulate recordings. While this approach produced an excellent record, Lhasa eventually found the endless tweaking both tedious and creatively unsatisfying. But using professional audiotape instead was expensive—too expensive for dawdling and unlimited recording. She and the band would be under pressure to come up with an acceptable live performance of any tune in three takes. It forced everyone to focus on giving fully realized live performances.

"The takes were intense, but the feeling wasn't rushed," says guitarist Joe Grass. "Sometimes I wasn't even sure if they were takes. But she would say, 'No, that's it.' For me, the surprise was how much space she kept in the music. My impulse was always to say we could do more, to want to overdub or add strings. And Lhasa would say, 'No, that's good.' I was very impressed with her. I had been working mostly with jazz musicians, but her intuition was spot-on. And I loved the way she sang."

Thierry Amar, an unusually sophisticated and iconoclastic musician in his own right, was also impressed. "I have to say that was an exceptional band and connection," he says. "She picked her people well and treated them well; she was able to defuse episodes quickly and was really good at that murky stuff. Technically, I don't think I changed a single mic position. It was effortless—take after take of pure, simple, flowing ideas. There were things Lhasa couldn't do on a technical level, but she had an ear. I found her chord changes profound: unexpected voicings and ideas. I had her behind me in the control room for all the vocal tracks and had to mute everything else so the music wouldn't hit the vocal mic. All I heard was her wonderful voice. Then I would play back the song and hear it for the first time with her and witness someone becoming the person she wants to be. What a voice she had."

Patrick Watson worked with her on several tracks. "She was having dilemmas with how dark her music was," he says. "I produced one song, 'Rising,' and I wanted to make it rise more." To do that, he proposed a variety of chord substitutions that gave the song a gentle, upward propulsion: Sarah's harp and Lhasa's voice spiraling in perfect synch with the lyrics, becoming ever lighter. Completely realized in conception and performance, it is one of Lhasa's great records and should, by all rights, have become a radio staple. But they struggled with another collaboration, "Where Do You Go," when Lhasa shocked Patrick by demonstrating her spine: though they were close friends and he had contributed the music for what was intended as a duet, Lhasa was never happy with any of Patrick's vocals, and she ultimately recorded the song without him. "She canned me!" Patrick says with a laugh. "'Hey! Ya can't fire me from the song I wrote!'" She certainly could—and did.

Lhasa also asked guitarist Freddy Koella—a player's player—to lend his touch to the record. Though French, he had lived for years in the United States and recorded and toured with a wide range of artists, including Bob Dylan, Willie DeVille, and k. d. lang. When Lhasa's band had been passing through Los Angeles a few years earlier, Rick and Mélanie had taken her to hear him play a club date. Lhasa later caught Freddy again at the Montreal Jazz Festival, and they struck up a friendship. There was no way he would decline to play on Lhasa's album—he adored her.

"She was obviously strong onstage, but in everyday life she was also strong and unique and funny," he says. "She was above. You know, sometimes you have a person in the medical field or philosophy and they are above the norm? She was above the norm musically. You would be in a room in Montreal with her and Watson and all those people and she was it. She was the light in the room."

Staying at Lhasa's house for a week, Koella got the full Montreal winter experience. "The plan was to walk to the studio," he says. "And one day there was a big storm—you couldn't see the cars parked on the street—and we still went by foot. What an expedition that was! It was fantastic, completely different than anything you could think of. And the other people were there already! It was freezing cold and when you open the studio door it's hot. We were wet like crawfish." None of which prevented him from laying down a moody, mysterious solo on "Love Came Here" and bringing a delicate, wistful resignation to the album's closing benediction, "Anyone & Everyone."

Thematically, many of the songs found Lhasa re-examining her notion of love. "She remained incredibly idealistic, but she was letting go of some fantasies of what her life could be and digging into the complexities of being in love," says Sarah. "Lhasa said that when you're in love and in a relationship and things are working, it's actually really a series of disappointments. And in some ways, that's true: when you start a relationship with somebody, it's all castles and clouds in the sky, and slowly possibilities get whittled away and whittled away. And at some point, you have to decide what's left—not just of your illusions but also of the reality of the situation and who you're with. Is it good enough? Is it something valuable and beautiful or is it all a big mistake? And that was a very difficult place for her to come to because I don't think she ever wanted to let go of the castles in the sky. And she was starting to."

The change in her views, says Ryan, was even more pronounced: "She was done with churning in her own solitary romantic suffering. She was really done with that."

Indeed, she was also re-examining the romantic views she had entertained regarding art and self-fulfillment. Once she had believed work and connecting with an audience would make her whole—that if she sacrificed and placed herself on the altar of art, all answers would flow. They had not. Now she was considering that those questions really had no answers but were best asked and understood by living life on its own daily terms. "She said, 'Look at Bob Dylan. He did everything, he's had a long career, and he's still depressed. Do we ever get out of this?'" recalls Ralph. "That stayed with me. That anguish—it doesn't have to do with success, money. It has to do with other things that can't be changed, only alleviated by acquiring some wisdom. It's one of the hardships of life."

The record emerging was, as Lhasa wished, musically straightforward. And if she intended it as a way to introduce herself to a wider American audience, there were several tracks, including "Fool's Gold," "Is Anything Wrong,"

"Love Came Here" and "Rising," that fit right in on American radio. But others, such as "Bells," "A Fish on Land," "The Lonely Spider," and "1001 Nights," have a sad, nearly mournful quality, while "I'm Going In," an extraordinary and deeply personal song about transfiguration and rebirth, was a stark reminder that Lhasa was no pop singer.

The record left executives at her label, Audiogram, unsure. They came to the studio as the album was nearing completion and told Lhasa the record was good but long, and some of the songs were too dark and heavy. They suggested the album would sell better if she left off certain tracks and began to tick off the ones she might consider removing. Lhasa cut them off.

"I'm sorry," she said. "Which of my children do you want me to kill?"

And that was the end of the meeting.

At home, Lhasa remained guarded about her condition. She gave out very little information, even to her family. There were a few months when she wasn't even sharing her status with them.

"Ayin and I would talk about it," says Samantha. "*What the fuck is she thinking?* Why isn't she calling these people and lighting a fire and getting her results? All Lhasa would say is, 'I have to figure it out for myself.' But Lhasa was always like that, even when she wasn't sick. She took her distance from the family; she took things into herself and took her space."

Finally, in early 2009, Lhasa began chemotherapy. It was every bit as awful as she had feared. "She got all the side effects," says Ryan. "It was fucking hellish." Somehow, though, she found a joke in it: one of the side effects was that her eyes were constantly tearing. "Look!" she would say with a laugh. "I'm *really* La Llorona now!"

Gallows humor came easily to her.

"I got incredibly sick," says Gabriela. "I had spinal meningitis and was in a hospital in Connecticut. "And Lhasa and I were talking to each other from our hospital beds. It was literally, 'Are we going to be okay?' 'I don't know—I'm in so much pain.' And then we would do cancer jokes and talk about how we were going to get people feeling sorry for us. And we would be in bed laughing our heads off."[1]

Alejandro and Marybeth would drive up from New York to see Lhasa. On a day she had chemotherapy, her father accompanied her and then drove her to the studio, where she worked on a vocal track. During a playback, she laid on the couch with her head in Sarah's lap. "An hour later, she opened her eyes and said, 'Oh, I must have fallen asleep!'" Alejandro recalls. "And then she went back to work."

Thierry watched Lhasa with a sense of wonder. "We were mixing the record in the spring and she was absolutely weaker," he says. "She would sleep behind me during the mixing and wake up for the listening. Her goal was to finish this record and I was kind of amazed. I thought we wouldn't finish it."

As bad as the side effects were, the chemotherapy was effective at halting the cancer. Buoyed by the results, she told friends and family that she was winning the battle, and she began laying out release plans for the new album, which she had decided to simply call *Lhasa*. She wanted to tour the United States. She really needed an American manager, but had no illusions that anyone would want to represent a woman battling cancer, so David-Etienne Savoie began acting as her temporary manager. To help promote her and the record, David hired the Brooklyn publicist Blake Zidell, who had worked with a long list of unique artists, including Laurie Anderson, Cecil Taylor, Ladysmith Black Mambazo, and Charlotte Gainsbourg. Concerts to debut the album were planned for theaters in Montreal and Paris, and Lhasa accepted a two-show booking in Reykjavik, Iceland, as a warm-up for a planned summer tour of Europe.

In April, Lhasa and her band performed for a group of friends at Patrick Watson's loft in the Mile End. Videotaped and edited into individual performance clips by the French documentarian Vincent Moon, who favored extreme close-ups, the results are like nothing ever shown on MTV. Dressed simply in jeans and a subtly spangled black top, Lhasa giggled between songs. But she didn't look like a girl anymore. Instead, there was a woman with short hair and marble white skin from chemotherapy. Her voice, once given to pyrotechnics, sounded fine and delicate. Almost miraculously, Lhasa stood unbroken and still singing. Only now it felt like she was singing herself into the next world.

Though its songs were all written prior to her diagnosis, *Lhasa* will be heard as a record of a death foretold. Perhaps it was simply Lhasa's brooding nature; perhaps her intuitiveness led her to suspect something was amiss—*what healthy young woman has the bones in her leg shatter?*—or perhaps her obsession with using universal archetypes simply led her to create wide-open songs easily given to multiple interpretations.

Most were songs of direct experience: "Bells" is about leaving Marseille and her boyfriend, Jerome. Yet, it has become impossible to hear it as anything but a dream of death, a plea for a story that "does not end this way." Packed with dark images of desolation and grief—of bells ringing through a drowned town, of birds flying upside down, of there being nothing left to do but surrender and "walk out there and go"—it comes to feel less like a breakup song and more like one of the surreal nightmare-scapes conjured in the unsettling films of Lhasa's favorite director, Andrei Tarkovsky.

Likewise, "A Fish on Land" is taken straight from one of Lhasa's dreams and animated by the cherished fairy tale trope that she embraced as a child in stories like "The Girl-Fish" and later loved to employ as an allegory in her art: the enchanted creature, the human in animal form who will be transformed and freed by love. Yet, there's nothing childlike about this dream; in fact, something feels ominously askew. To help the gasping fish with a human face, whom she recognizes as her husband-to-be, she needs to place him in water but can only submerge him in a puddle that doesn't seem life-giving or inviting at all, "a grey and still and dusty thing." The fish becomes a man and they marry, but there's no sense of joy. The image that lingers at song's end is still of a fish on land gasping for breath. "Is life like this for everyone? / Is life like this for everyone?"

Most obviously unsettling, however, is the tour de force, "I'm Going In." Written years earlier, it had been composed as a song about being born and reborn. Deeply, religiously hopeful, it brims with Lhasa's optimism and faith that she can never truly be obliterated, that "even lost and blind / I still invented love." All that would be overshadowed by the song's awful prescience:

I'll be falling by the wayside,
You'll be holding out your hand.
Don't you tempt me with perfection,
I have other things to do.
I didn't burrow this far in,
Just to come right back to you.

Erik West-Millette, who had known Lhasa first as a twenty-one-year-old waitress who wanted to sing Billie Holiday songs, stood against the wall at Patrick Watson's and listened with foreboding as his friend sang her own songs. Afterward, he gave her a big hug, while urging her to postpone her tour. "Just go in six months," he told her. "Take the time to be strong." But he knew her well enough to know that wasn't going to happen. "She said, 'No, no, no—I have to do this.' And I was not surprised that she didn't survive."

With both the future and her continued ability to protect her body from major medical procedures less and less certain, Lhasa felt the clock ticking: motherhood, which had loomed for years as an unanswered question, now became desperately important. And when Ryan said he wasn't sure he wanted to be a father, Lhasa made the choice clear: with or without him, she was going to become a mother—and as soon as possible.

Her separation from Ryan all but sealed, her personal life and health in a tumult, Lhasa continued to work. The next month, she and the band played a pair of concerts to debut the album, one at Montreal's Corona Theater, the other in Paris at the Theater Bouffes du Nord. In Paris, Lhasa had a chance to see her mother, with whom she had made up. "It got a lot better," Alexandra says. "There were lots of joking emails back and forth and we had a nice time in Paris."

From France, Lhasa, Joe, and Sarah traveled to London for a round of promotion that included an on-air performance on the BBC with Charlie Gillett at which they played an impromptu version of Sam Cooke's psalm "A Change Is Gonna Come." The band was reunited in Iceland, where they rented a house. Hearing Joe working up a chord progression, Lhasa began singing along. "I like this," she said. "We should do something."

Onstage in Reykjavik, Lhasa seemed relaxed and in fine voice, joking with the audience between songs.[2] "It was incredible how focused she could be and the joy she could convey," Joe says. The band was caught off guard at the end of the second show when Lhasa bowed with them, waved to the audience and smiled, walked offstage, and burst into tears.

"It was a great show, but she felt like she was giving away too much onstage and that there wasn't enough left for her," says Sarah. Until that moment, Lhasa had never shown her musicians anything but an unswerving belief that her health would improve and that they would achieve everything they had planned. "But, of course, she knew that wasn't the case."

She hadn't been back in Montreal three days when she showed up at a rehearsal with most of the lyrics for "Island Song,"[3] the tune she and Joe had begun. Later in the week, when Sarah and Joe accompanied her on a CBC broadcast to promote the album, she insisted on including the new song. A few days later, the trio recorded a finished version. It proved Lhasa's final recording.

In June, Sarah and Lhasa got together to rehearse for an upcoming private show as a duo. After a few minutes, Lhasa said she had a headache and had to lie down. That week, she began to have seizures. The cancer had metastasized; brain tumors were causing cerebral edema.

"Up to that point, I think she really thought she would live," says Eden. "She definitely held it together super, super well for a lot of the time. She thought, *Okay, this is really hard, but I'm going to make it.*"

"It was frustrating and terrible," says Marybeth. "I think she might still be alive if she had handled it differently, but I don't know. You never know. It was a virulent cancer and very powerful. And when you're a young woman, it tends to be ferocious; the survivors are usually post-menopausal women."

In August, Lhasa called Alexandra and asked her to come back to Montreal.

"She had done the chemo and asked me to help her do the Gerson Cancer Diet," she says. "Which is a very strict diet—a lot of vegetable juices and so forth. So I went in the summer and stayed. When I was with her that time, it was completely different. We were very close at that point."

In an effort to shrink the tumors and kill the cancer cells, Lhasa also underwent radiotherapy, receiving high doses of radiation. Still a vibrant dreamer, she dreamed one night that she was lying outside under an enormous night sky with Ayin, Sky, and Miriam when she saw something moving out of the heavens and toward them. "What's that thing?" she asked, pointing up into the darkness. But no one else could see it. Frightened, she woke up.

She continued her own daily regimen. "She was meditating a lot," says Alejandro. "Eating only organic food—

juice mostly. She would get up every morning and come down and open the windows and pull the blinds and feed her plants. And then take to the mats—almost every day sitting out on the patio—and begin her yoga practice. When she was doing the radiation treatments she had no hair and she would put blue mud on her face because she felt it would extract the badness of the radiation treatments. So she was bald and blue, sitting on her patio engaged in yoga and surrounded by her friends and family."

Dan Seligman, a concert promoter and neighbor, could tell the situation was grim. Yet, Lhasa managed to sound upbeat if he came by to look in on her. Indeed, when Seligman told Lhasa that he and his wife had just discovered they were going to be parents again—something they hadn't planned on—she responded with a mischievous twinkle. "I guess your daughter had her own plan," she said.

As autumn crept up on Montreal, a steady stream of sisters flowed through the house—not just Eden but Gabriela from Brooklyn, Samantha from Oregon, and the other "quadruplets" from France—as everyone held their breath.

"None of us thought this could happen—there's no cancer in our family," says Gabriela. "It was bad and then worse and worse. It took on a nightmarish quality where every single test you take is positive for cancer. It's in your lungs. It's in your liver. It's in your bones. It's in your lymph nodes. Every single test. It was epically terrible. *What's happening?*"

Yet Lhasa could still flash something of her old self. "If we were about to go out for a bit, Lhasa would say,

'Remember to put on some lipstick and let your hair down and flirt a little!'" says Samantha. "And she would do that little giggle thing and we would laugh and my mom and sisters and I would go for a walk around the block to get some air or go to the bagel store or something. And I also remember Lhasa saying, 'Our bodies are so generous.' Her body was leaving her and yet she was saying this."

One night Lhasa's friend Ralph was even able to convince her to leave the house. "I took her to a restaurant she liked in Chinatown," he says. "I remember it very well and will never forget. She hadn't eaten a lot—the smell in the restaurant was making her nauseous. We were going to the car, walking in silence. And she looked at me and said, 'At the end of the day, what is it? More of the same. So if I live to be eighty or I die now, it's really more of the same.'"

Ryan, who had remained with Lhasa following her seizures, saw the change in her. "I was utterly, utterly convinced in her recovery," he says. "I never in my solitary moments ever questioned her survival even once until about mid-November when she had no will. For the first time in this whole journey, I realized that she might not survive. I can say that now, but at the time I was fucking steadfast."

Receiving little information, friends were unsure what to do. Bïa, who had been in Brazil for six months, wanted to introduce Lhasa to her new son. When she couldn't get an answer to her emails, she assumed Lhasa was busy. "I didn't know the cancer had come back furiously," she said.

"I wouldn't just come and barge in, but Erik was saying, 'No, Lhasa is going to leave us. If you want to see her, go there.' And I didn't want to hear that. *Are you crazy? She's going to be okay!* So I have this regret that I couldn't be there more for her. Also, I don't know if I was welcome. Because there were people there—her mother, her sisters. I had this feeling that it was more I wanted to see her and show her that I loved her. But she knew I loved her. Yeah."

"We were not allowed to say goodbye," says Patrick. "It leaves it raw."

"There had to be no doubt in the people around her," says her brother Mischa. "It was what she required, all the way to the end."

When Alexandra called a hospice service, they sent someone to discuss their program. Lhasa, sitting with her mother, heard the woman repeatedly use the phrase "palliative care" and burst into tears. Alexandra quickly put an end to the visit, walking the rep to the door. "Don't use that term again," she said.

Instead, Alexandra called Isabel Lalonde, a nurse and the wife of Lhasa's drummer and producer, François. "She said Lhasa is coming to the end and she wants Isabel to be her nurse," François says. "And my wife accepted this."

Lhasa's brain tumors continued to strip her bit by bit. Along with the seizures, she began to have hallucinations. "I would just play along," says Ralph. "She would say, 'I see a cat walking along the wall,' and giggle. So I would see the cat, too."

Gabriela drove up from New York every ten days through November and December.

"My mother and Ryan were there with her," she says. "I would sleep in bed with Lhasa at the end of her life when she was blind and couldn't walk. Because she was restless, in a sort of unconscious way. I remember she sat up one night in the middle of the night and she turned her body and just laid her head down on my stomach like I was her pillow and went back to sleep. She might or might not have had any idea what she was doing at that point. But I remember it. I don't know if there is value in watching someone that you love suffer so horribly. I don't think there's value in it. And that's my takeaway. I wish *like hell* that she had decided to end her life by her own choice several months earlier rather than go through what she went through. I wish that."

Lhasa de Sela died at home on New Year's Day 2010, just before midnight.

It was already early morning in France when Alexandra began making calls. Ayin, crossing the field to Sky's house at dawn, found her sister awake. "She did her greatest magic trick," said Sky. "She disappeared."[4]

Three days later, David-Etienne Savoie would release news of her passing. "It has snowed more than forty hours in Montreal since Lhasa's departure," he wrote.

Those who remained still felt her presence. The night before Lhasa died, her bassist, Miles Perkins, had a dream.

"I was in a car and a song of hers came on the radio," he said. "And I just wanted to sit in the car and listen until it ended. Then I flipped the radio off and got out, and woke up. Two days later I got the news."[5]

"When she died, something in the world died for me," says Patrick, who requested and received as a keepsake the blanket Lhasa kept over her television. "Some people play at the Gypsy world as theater—it's kind of like watching a fake movie. But Lhasa was the real thing and the last that I knew. When she passed, that feeling died with her. And the world changed."

"My daughters love her music," says Freddy Koella. "I tell them all the time, 'It's a bad thing that you can't meet her.'"

For Lousnak, Lhasa's death ripped the seams from her own life: "When she passed away, I was in nine months of therapy. I had never had anybody close to me die like that and when my daughter left home at the same time I thought I was losing it. Do you know that line written a long time ago: *when a tree falls in the forest does anyone hear it?* Lhasa knew me so well—so now, without her, I'm wondering, *do I still exist?* Of all my friends, she was the one who got me. I can't even say that for my husband then or my boyfriend now. And this is what I think of when I think about her. It's almost unbearable. Maybe in ten years I can tell you something different but right now I still can't bear her absence. Still, sometimes, it's like a lack of oxygen, a claustrophobia. Because you can't find her anywhere. After her I'm more careful about who I love—it's terrible!"

"Her absence defines my understanding of life," says Ralph. "Paraphrasing Jacques Brel, *if I were God I wouldn't be too proud of myself today.*"[6]

Still, he witnessed something he couldn't forget: Alexandra, who had brought Lhasa into the world and named her—had loved her and taught her and inspired her and hurt her and been hurt in turn but ultimately and at last finding each other and all of that always in the name of life—holding fast to her daughter.

"I call Alexandra the mother of all mothers," Ralph says. "I've never seen anything like that. My mom would have died, simply. Alexandra was a model of everything. Everything. She's somebody who knows life very well and herself very well. And the way she dealt with the death of her beloved daughter—because Lhasa was her beloved daughter—was more than heroic. It was a true lesson. And she did it with such focus and such discipline. Without making anyone around her feel she was to be pitied."

Following her daughter's passing, Alexandra returned to Marseille. In 2014, the City of Montreal built a children's park where Mile End meets Little Italy and dedicated it in Lhasa's name. Friends performed; Alejandro spoke. The following year Alexandra, now in her mid-seventies, returned to Montreal and its long winter and took an apartment within walking distance of the park. Sarah Pagé, Ralph Dfouni, Ryan Morey, and Patrick Watson are among those who come to be with her in the living room filled with paintings and photographs and music and books. "She's a real something," says Patrick. "I still don't know what yet. She's been places and knows what's going on. Sometimes I spend time with her so I can feel like I'm hanging out with Lhasa."

As the first shocks subsided, Gabriela and Samantha saw the world through changed eyes.

"The one thing I will say about going through that," says Gabriela, "is that if you love someone and go through that process with them you instantly become part of the larger family of man. It makes you aware of what people suffer and go through in life. I had no idea until this happened; I was completely ignorant. And now I understand."

"I was flying back and forth between here and Montreal to take care of her," says Samantha. "A friend had given me a statue of a weeping carved Buddha. In the times between being with her I would do my meditation in the morning and sob. We just kept getting worse and worse news. It was excruciating: like sliding down a razor blade. I wanted my body to curl up; everybody in our family was in so much pain.

"And I remember Lhasa having breakfast with Sky one morning and saying, 'I guess I just have to say yes to whatever comes.' Even if it was her death. And I have remembered that. I do my meditation and I stand up and I open my arms and I open my chest and I say, 'Yes.' And I have done that ever since."

POSTSCRIPT

"The Girl-Fish": A Catalonian Folktale
as Recounted by Andrew Lang in
The Orange Fairy Book

Once upon a time there lived, on the bank of a stream, a
man and a woman who had a daughter. As she was an only
child, and very pretty besides, they never could make up
their minds to punish her for her faults or to teach her nice
manners; and as for work—she laughed in her mother's
face if she asked her to help cook the dinner or to wash the
plates. All the girl would do was to spend her days in dancing and playing with her friends; and for any use she was
to her parents they might as well have no daughter at all.

However, one morning her mother looked so tired that
even the selfish girl could not help seeing it, and asked if
there was anything she was able to do, so that her mother
might rest a little.

The good woman looked so surprised and grateful
for this offer that the girl felt rather ashamed, and at that
moment would have scrubbed down the house if she had
been requested; but her mother only begged her to take
the fishing-net out to the bank of the river and mend some
holes in it, as her father intended to go fishing that night.

The girl took the net and worked so hard that soon there was not a hole to be found. She felt quite pleased with herself, though she had had plenty to amuse her, as everybody who passed by had stopped and had a chat with her. But by this time the sun was high overhead, and she was just folding her net to carry it home again, when she heard a splash behind her, and looking round she saw a big fish jump into the air. Seizing the net with both hands, she flung it into the water where the circles were spreading one behind the other, and, more by luck than skill, drew out the fish.

"Well, you are a beauty!" she cried to herself; but the fish looked up to her and said:

"You had better not kill me, for, if you do, I will turn you into a fish yourself!"

The girl laughed contemptuously, and ran straight in to her mother.

"Look what I have caught," she said gaily; "but it is almost a pity to eat it, for it can talk, and it declares that, if I kill it, it will turn me into a fish too."

"Oh, put it back, put it back!" implored the mother. "Perhaps it is skilled in magic. And I should die, and so would your father, if anything should happen to you."

"Oh, nonsense, mother; what power could a creature like that have over me? Besides, I am hungry, and if I don't have my dinner soon, I shall be cross." And off she went to gather some flowers to stick in her hair.

About an hour later the blowing of a horn told her that dinner was ready.

"Didn't I say that fish would be delicious?" she cried; and plunging her spoon into the dish the girl helped herself to a large piece. But the instant it touched her mouth a cold shiver ran through her. Her head seemed to flatten, and her eyes to look oddly round the corners; her legs and her arms were stuck to her sides, and she gasped wildly for breath. With a mighty bound she sprang through the window and fell into the river, where she soon felt better, and was able to swim to the sea, which was close by.

No sooner had she arrived there than the sight of her sad face attracted the notice of some of the other fishes, and they pressed round her, begging her to tell them her story.

"I am not a fish at all," said the new-comer, swallowing a great deal of salt water as she spoke; for you cannot learn how to be a proper fish all in a moment. "I am not a fish at all, but a girl; at least I was a girl a few minutes ago, only—" And she ducked her head under the waves so that they should not see her crying.

"Only you did not believe that the fish you caught had power to carry out its threat," said an old tunny. "Well, never mind, that has happened to all of us, and it really is not a bad life. Cheer up and come with us and see our queen, who lives in a palace that is much more beautiful than any your queens can boast of."

The new fish felt a little afraid of taking such a journey; but as she was still more afraid of being left alone, she waved her tail in token of consent, and off they all set, hundreds of them together. The people on the rocks and in the ships that saw them pass said to each other: "Look what a splendid shoal!" and had no idea that they were hastening to the queen's palace; but, then, dwellers on land have so little notion of what goes on in the bottom of the sea! Certainly the little new fish had none. She had watched jelly-fish and nautilus swimming a little way below the surface, and beautiful colored sea-weeds floating about; but that was all. Now, when she plunged deeper her eyes fell upon strange things.

Wedges of gold, great anchors, heaps of pearl, inestimable stones, unvalued jewels—all scattered in the bottom of the sea! Dead men's bones were there also, and long white creatures who had never seen the light, for they mostly dwelt in the clefts of rocks where the sun's rays could not come. At first our little fish felt as if she were blind also, but by-and-by she began to make out one object after another in the green dimness, and by the time she had swum for a few hours all became clear.

"Here we are at last," cried a big fish, going down into a deep valley, for the sea has its mountains and valleys just as much as the land. "That is the palace of the queen of the fishes, and I think you must confess that the emperor himself has nothing so fine."

"It is beautiful indeed," gasped the little fish, who was very tired with trying to swim as fast as the rest, and beautiful beyond words the palace was. The walls were made of pale pink coral, worn smooth by the waters, and round the windows were rows of pearls; the great doors were standing open, and the whole troop floated into the chamber of audience, where the queen, who was half a woman after all, was seated on a throne made of a green and blue shell.

"Who are you, and where do you come from?" said she to the little fish, whom the others had pushed in front. And in a low, trembling voice, the visitor told her story.

"I was once a girl too," answered the queen, when the fish had ended; "and my father was the king of a great country. A husband was found for me, and on my wedding-day my mother placed her crown on my head and told me that as long as I wore it I should likewise be queen. For many months I was as happy as a girl could be, especially when I had a little son to play with. But, one morning, when I was walking in my gardens, there came a giant and snatched the crown from my head. Holding me fast, he told me that he intended to give the crown to his daughter, and to enchant my husband the prince, so that he should not know the difference between us. Since then she has filled my place and been queen in my stead. As for me, I was so miserable that I threw myself into the sea, and my ladies, who loved me, declared that they would die too; but, instead of dying, some wizard, who pitied my fate, turned us all into fishes, though he allowed me to keep the face and body of a woman. And fishes we must remain till someone brings me back my crown again!"

"I will bring it back if you tell me what to do!" cried the little fish, who would have promised anything that was likely to carry her up to earth again. And the queen answered:

"Yes, I will tell you what to do."

She sat silent for a moment, and then went on:

"There is no danger if you will only follow my counsel; and first you must return to earth, and go up to the top of a high mountain, where the giant has built his castle. You will find him sitting on the steps weeping for his daughter, who has just died while the prince was away hunting. At the last she sent her father my crown by a faithful servant. But I warn you to be careful, for if he sees you he may kill you. Therefore I will give you the power to change yourself into any creature that may help you best. You have only to strike your forehead, and call out its name."

This time the journey to land seemed much shorter than before, and when once the fish reached the shore she struck her forehead sharply with her tail, and cried:

"Deer, come to me!"

In a moment the small, slimy body disappeared, and in its place stood a beautiful beast with branching horns and slender legs, quivering with longing to be gone. Throwing back her head and snuffing the air, she broke into a run, leaping easily over the rivers and walls that stood in her way.

It happened that the king's son had been hunting since daybreak, but had killed nothing, and when the deer crossed his path as he was resting under a tree he determined to have her. He flung himself on his horse, which went like the wind, and as the prince had often hunted the forest before, and knew all the short cuts, he at last came up with the panting beast.

"By your favor let me go, and do not kill me," said the deer, turning to the prince with tears in her eyes, "for I have far to run and much to do." And as the prince, struck dumb with surprise, only looked at her, the deer cleared the next wall and was soon out of sight.

"That can't really be a deer," thought the prince to himself, reining in his horse and not attempting to follow her. "No deer ever had eyes like that. It must be an enchanted maiden, and I will marry her and no other." So, turning his horse's head, he rode slowly back to his palace.

The deer reached the giant's castle quite out of breath, and her heart sank as she gazed at the tall, smooth walls which surrounded it. Then she plucked up courage and cried:

"Ant, come to me!" And in a moment the branching horns and beautiful shape had vanished, and a tiny brown ant, invisible to all who did not look closely, was climbing up the walls.

It was wonderful how fast she went, that little creature! The wall must have appeared miles high in comparison with her own body; yet, in less time than would have seemed possible, she was over the top and down in the courtyard on the other side. Here she paused to consider what had best be done next, and looking about her she saw that one of the walls had a tall tree growing by it, and in the corner was a window very nearly on a level with the highest branches of the tree.

"Monkey, come to me!" cried the ant; and before you could turn round a monkey was swinging herself from the topmost branches into the room where the giant lay snoring.

"Perhaps he will be so frightened at the sight of me that he may die of fear, and I shall never get the crown," thought the monkey. "I had better become something else." And she called softly: "Parrot, come to me!"

Then a pink and grey parrot hopped up to the giant, who by this time was stretching himself and giving yawns which shook the castle. The parrot waited a little, until he was really awake, and then she said boldly that she had been sent to take away the crown, which was not his any longer, now his daughter the queen was dead.

On hearing these words the giant leapt out of bed with an angry roar, and sprang at the parrot in order to wring her neck with his great hands. But the bird was too quick for him, and, flying behind his back, begged the giant to have patience, as her death would be of no use to him.

"That is true," answered the giant; "but I am not so foolish as to give you that crown for nothing. Let me think what I will have in exchange!" And he scratched his huge head for several minutes, for giants' minds always move slowly.

"Ah, yes, that will do!" exclaimed the giant at last, his face brightening. "You shall have the crown if you will bring me a collar of blue stones from the Arch of St. Martin, in the Great City."

Now when the parrot had been a girl she had often heard of this wonderful arch and the precious stones and marbles that had been let into it. It sounded as if it would be a very hard thing to get them away from the building of which they formed a part, but all had gone well with her so far, and at any rate she could but try. So she bowed to the giant, and made her way back to the window where the giant could not see her. Then she called quickly:

"Eagle, come to me!"

Before she had even reached the tree she felt herself borne up on strong wings ready to carry her to the clouds if she wished to go there, and seeming a mere speck in the sky, she was swept along till she beheld the Arch of St. Martin far below, with the rays of the sun shining on it. Then she swooped down, and, hiding herself behind a buttress so that she could not be detected from below, she set herself to dig out the nearest blue stones with her beak. It was even harder work than she had expected; but at last it was done, and hope arose in her heart. She next drew out a piece of string that she had found hanging from a tree, and sitting down to rest strung the stones together. When the necklace was finished she hung it round her neck, and called: "Parrot, come to me!" And a little later the pink and grey parrot stood before the giant.

"Here is the necklace you asked for," said the parrot. And the eyes of the giant glistened as he took the heap of blue stones in his hand. But for all that he was not minded to give up the crown.

"They are hardly as blue as I expected," he grumbled, though the parrot knew as well as he did that he was not speaking the truth; "so you must bring me something else in exchange for the crown you covet so much. If you fail it will cost you not only the crown but your life also."

"What is it you want now?" asked the parrot; and the giant answered:

"If I give you my crown I must have another still more beautiful; and this time you shall bring me a crown of stars."

The parrot turned away, and as soon as she was outside she murmured:

"Toad, come to me!" And sure enough a toad she was, and off she set in search of the starry crown.

She had not gone far before she came to a clear pool, in which the stars were reflected so brightly that they looked quite real to touch and handle. Stooping down she filled a bag she was carrying with the shining water and, returning to the castle, wove a crown out of the reflected stars. Then she cried as before:

"Parrot, come to me!" And in the shape of a parrot she entered the presence of the giant.

"Here is the crown you asked for," she said; and this time the giant could not help crying out with admiration. He knew he was beaten, and still holding the chaplet of stars, he turned to the girl.

"Your power is greater than mine: take the crown; you have won it fairly!"

The parrot did not need to be told twice. Seizing the crown, she sprang on to the window, crying: "Monkey, come to me!" And to a monkey, the climb down the tree into the courtyard did not take half a minute. When she had reached the ground she said again: "Ant, come to me!" And a little ant at once began to crawl over the high wall. How glad the ant was to be out of the giant's castle, holding fast the crown which had shrunk into almost nothing, as she herself had done, but grew quite big again when the ant exclaimed:

"Deer, come to me!"

Surely no deer ever ran so swiftly as that one! On and on she went, bounding over rivers and crashing through tangles till she reached the sea. Here she cried for the last time:

"Fish, come to me!" And, plunging in, she swam along the bottom as far as the palace, where the queen and all the fishes gathered together awaiting her.

The hours since she had left had gone very slowly—as they always do to people that are waiting—and many of them had quite given up hope.

"I am tired of staying here," grumbled a beautiful little creature, whose colors changed with every movement of her body, "I want to see what is going on in the upper world. It must be months since that fish went away."

"It was a very difficult task, and the giant must certainly have killed her or she would have been back long ago," remarked another.

"The young flies will be coming out now," murmured a third, "and they will all be eaten up by the river fish! It is really too bad!" When, suddenly, a voice was heard from behind: "Look! Look! What is that bright thing that is moving so swiftly towards us?" And the queen started up, and stood on her tail, so excited was she.

A silence fell on all the crowd, and even the grumblers held their peace and gazed like the rest.

On and on came the fish, holding the crown tightly in her mouth, and the others moved back to let her pass. On she went right up to the queen, who bent and, taking the crown, placed it on her own head. Then a wonderful thing happened. Her tail dropped away or, rather, it divided and grew into two legs and a pair of the prettiest feet in the world, while her maidens, who were grouped around her, shed their scales and became girls again. They all turned and looked at each other first, and next at the little fish who had regained her own shape and was more beautiful than any of them.

"It is you who have given us back our life; you, you!" they cried; and fell to weeping from very joy.

So they all went back to earth and the queen's palace, and quite forgot the one that lay under the sea. But they had been so long away that they found many changes. The prince, the queen's husband, had died some years since, and in his place was her son, who had grown up and was king! Even in his joy at seeing his mother again an air of sadness clung to him, and at last the queen could bear it no longer, and begged him to walk with her in the garden. Seated together in a bower of jessamine—where she had passed long hours as a bride—she took her son's hand and entreated him to tell her the cause of his sorrow. "For," said she, "if I can give you happiness you shall have it."

"It is no use," answered the prince; "nobody can help me. I must bear it alone."

"But at least let me share your grief," urged the queen.

"No one can do that," said he. "I have fallen in love with what I can never marry, and I must get on as best I can."

"It may not be as impossible as you think," answered the queen. "At any rate, tell me."

There was silence between them for a moment, then, turning away his head, the prince answered gently:

"I have fallen in love with a beautiful deer!"

"Ah, if that is all," exclaimed the queen joyfully. And she told him in broken words that, as he had guessed, it was no deer but an enchanted maiden who had won back the crown and brought her home to her own people.

"She is here, in my palace," added the queen. "I will take you to her."

But when the prince stood before the girl, who was so much more beautiful than anything he had ever dreamed of, he lost all his courage, and stood with bent head before her.

Then the maiden drew near, and her eyes, as she looked at him, were the eyes of the deer that day in the forest. She whispered softly:

"By your favor let me go, and do not kill me."

And the prince remembered her words, and his heart was filled with happiness. And the queen, his mother, watched them and smiled.

ACKNOWLEDGMENTS

In December 2017, Lhasa's friends and family marked the twentieth anniversary of the release of her debut album, *La Llorona*, with concerts in Paris and Montreal. The latter was an opportunity for me to spend several days meeting and interviewing many of her friends and musical collaborators. It also provided a bit of a reality check: in the United States, Lhasa is still largely unknown, and every conversation I have about her invariably begins with a description of who she was, what her records sound like, and why she moves me enough to want to write a book about her. But on a frigid winter night just forty miles north of the border she had no trouble selling out the twenty-three hundred tickets at MTelus concert hall. Seven years after her death, Lhasa continued to be an icon in her adopted hometown.

She is also very much a spiritual presence, as I quickly discovered in my conversations with her friends and sidemen. The passage of time notwithstanding, her death remains tender and still something of a shock to many of them.

My gratitude first and foremost to Lhasa's family/tribe in all its incarnations—the Selas, de Selas, de la Vegas, Karams, and Pettits—for sharing so many lovely and sometimes painful memories. I want to especially thank both her parents, Alejandro and Alexandra, who invited me into their homes with warmth and grace and spoke to me without conditions. Their influence on their daughter and her life and work is nearly incalculable, and this book is as much about them and their choices as it is about Lhasa. A special thank you to Lhasa's brother Mischa, who administers her business in Montreal, for making my task so straightforward and enjoyable.

I am similarly indebted to Lhasa's friends and collaborators, both in Montreal and Europe, for sharing their recollections and impressions. A special shout-out to filmmaker Nanna Frank Møller for providing a copy of *Someone Like You*, her moving film about Ayin and Sky de Sela and their lives as circus performers and sisters.

Stephen Hull, at the University Press of New England, invited me to write this book and got the Music Matters series rolling before it came to land (but not rest!) at its ultimate home at the University of Texas Press. I'm similarly indebted to the series' editor, Evelyn McDonnell, for her enthusiasm and feedback.

Working with Casey Kittrell, an acquisitions editor at the UT Press, has been an unexpected treat—I hope this is just "hello." Thanks also to his aide-de-camp, Andrew Hnatow, for help in ferrying me through the process. Copyeditor Sally Furgeson's sharp pencil and enthusiasm for Lhasa greatly enhanced the telling of this story. My deep thanks to the people at the University of Texas Press who turned this manuscript into a book and put it into your hands: Joel Pinckney, Cameron Ludwick, Bailey Morrison, Gianna LaMorte, Bob Barnett, and Cassandra Cisneros. And I'm personally touched by the work of Dustin Kilgore, who designed the text, and Amanda Weiss, who created a book cover conveying Lhasa's spirit.

Early readers and lifelong bleeders: David Booth, Jeffrey Bumiller, Crescenzo Capece, Paul Feinman, Janet Goodman, Joshua Goodman, Eddie Karp, Sam Sutherland, and Jim Whelan. A big *merci* to Cathy Booth for helping with French translations.

As usual, Lhasa put it best: *There is no end to this story.*

NOTES

Unless otherwise noted, all quotations are from original interviews conducted between August 2017 and April 2018.

Chapter 1: A Flock of Black Sheep

1. Peter Culshaw, "World Music's Discovery of the Year," *Telegraph*, November 25, 2004.
2. R. Gordon Wasson, "Seeking the Magic Mushroom," *Life*, June 10, 1957. Wasson played a large part in introducing the world to psychedelic mushrooms. He made numerous subsequent trips to the village to observe the ceremony, including one with the French mycologist Roger Heim, who in turn sent samples of the mushroom to Albert Hofmann, the Swiss chemist who created LSD. Hofmann isolated the active ingredient and created synthetic psilocybin for clinical use. Wasson would later express regrets about the broad public use of psychedelics and the way his article had pointed a path to Sabina's door, creating problems with the authorities for the shaman, her village, and their way of life.
3. Alejandro Sela de Obarrio, "Lhasa's Best Birthday," unpublished essay/ remembrance.
4. Interview with Cédric Edouard, 1998, www.sendereando.com (Lhasa tribute site).
5. *She Moves between Two Worlds*, CBC Radio documentary, written and produced by Madonna Hamel, originally aired on *Inside the Music with Patty Schmidt*, January 2011.
6. Ibid.
7. Ibid.
8. Ibid.
9. Dan Hilborn, "The Amazing Life of Lhasa," *Burnaby Now*, July 25, 2005.
10. *Someone Like You*, directed by Hanna Frank Møller, 2006.

11. Interview with Cédric Edouard, 1998, www.sendereando.com (Lhasa tribute site).

12. Peter Culshaw, "Lhasa de Sela, 1972–2010," *BBC Arts Desk*, January 5, 2010.

Chapter 2: The Wailing Woman

1. Les Foufounes Électriques is a popular music club in Montreal's Latin Quarter.

2. *La Route de Lhasa*, radio documentary produced by Elise Andrieu, originally aired on "Une Vie, Une Oeuvre," *French Culture*, 2010.

3. Christine Charter, "Tales of the Road," *fRoots*, April 1, 2004.

4. Stefan Christoff, "Cultural Crossroads: In Lhasa's World," *The Hour*, August 13, 2009.

5. Fake books are large compendiums featuring the chords and melodies to popular tunes and standards—basically, lead sheets for musicians who play weddings and other formal events where they must play a wide range of music.

6. Tenochtitlán was the Aztec city-state on whose ruins rose Mexico City.

7. Interview with Malachy O'Neill, BBC, September 6, 2009.

8. Interview with Jacki Lyden, *All Things Considered*, NPR, 1998.

9. Jamie O'Meara, "Lhasa de Sela Loses Fight With Cancer; Montreal Mourns the Loss of the Remarkable Lhasa de Sela," *The Hour*, January 7, 2010.

10. Malachy O'Neill, review of *The Living Road*, BBC, 2004.

Chapter 3: The Paradox

1. Ann Powers, "Extolling Femininity, Gently," *New York Times*, June 22, 1998.

2. Christine Charter, "Tales of the Road," *fRoots*, April 1, 2004.

3. Peter Culshaw, "World Music's Discovery of the Year," *Telegraph*, November 25, 2004.

4. Stefan Christoff, "Cultural Crossroads: In Lhasa's World," *The Hour*, August 13, 2009.

5. Culshaw, "World Music's Discovery."

6. Philly Markowitz, "Back to Lhasa," *Roots World*, 2004.

7. Three Kings' Day, celebrated in Spain and many of its former colonies, falls on the twelfth day of Christmas and commemorates the visit of Caspar, Melchior, and Balthazar to the baby Jesus.

8. Markowitz, "Back to Lhasa."

9. Malachy O'Neill, "RIP Lhasa," January 12, 2010, www.charliegillet.com.

10. *She Moves between Two Worlds*, CBC Radio documentary, written and produced by Madonna Hamel, originally aired on *Inside the Music with Patty Schmidt*, January 2011.

11. Peter Culshaw, "Lhasa de Sela, 1972–2010," *BBC Arts Desk*, January 5, 2010.

12. Scorpion is a card game akin to solitaire.

13. Interview with Malachy O'Neill, BBC, September 6, 2009.

14. Ibid.

Chapter 4: Mile End

1. Christine Charter, "Tales of the Road," *fRoots*, April 1, 2004. In a telling and humorous exchange about the song, journalist Christine Charter asked Lhasa if by "men" she was speaking of mankind in general or men in particular. "I mean men!" she exclaimed with a laugh.

2. Ibid.

3. "A Torch Singer with an Ancient Sound," *New York Times*, June 4, 2005.

4. At the bottom of the BBC Radio 3 page profiling Lhasa as the winner of the Americas Award is a long list of comments and praise from listeners in two dozen countries. Near the bottom is a submission more personal than the others: "I love her and I'm grateful for her sage brave gifts of music and poetry. Gracias, m'hija.—Alejandro Sela, West Sand Lake, NY."

5. Peter Culshaw, "World Music's Discovery of the Year," *Telegraph*, November 25, 2004.

6. Robin Denselow, "Lhasa: The Living Road," *Guardian*, January 22, 2004.

7. *La Route de Lhasa*, radio documentary produced by Elise Andrieu, originally aired on "Une Vie, Une Oeuvre," *French Culture*, 2010.

8. *The Fortean Times*, published in the United Kingdom, bills itself as the

"World's Weirdest News." It has its origins in the work of Charles Fort, an early twentieth-century American science skeptic and novelist who focused on unexplained phenomena. Fort argued that science cannot explain all occurrences.

9. Jason Heller, "Stuart A. Staples on Tindersticks' 'The Waiting Room,' Track by Track," *All Songs Considered*, National Public Radio, January 14, 2016.

10. Will Hermes, "MultiCult Records: Latin American Art-Folk Isn't 'World Music,' It's Plain Weird," *Spin*, December 1998.

11. Sasha Frere-Jones, "Critic's Notebook: Around the World," *New Yorker*, October 10, 2005.

12. Although she never added a cello to the new band, Lhasa was likely thinking of cellist Sam Shalabi, a musician associated with several adventurous groups including Thee Silver Mt. Zion Memorial Orchestra. Lhasa appeared at about this time on his album *Eid*, contributing a very un-Lhasa-like vocal on "End Game."

Chapter 5: Bells

1. In a terrible coincidence, Ayin developed a brain aneurysm around the same time. She lost her sense of balance, ending her career as a high-wire artist.

2. An album culled from these shows was released in 2017 as *Live in Reykjavik*.

3. The Icelandic spelling for Iceland is "Island."

4. *La Route de Lhasa*, radio documentary produced by Elise Andrieu, originally aired on "Une Vie, Une Oeuvre," *French Culture*, 2010.

5. Ibid.

6. Ibid.